DATE DUE

~~JUN 3 0 1995~~	

How Young Children Perceive Race

SAGE SERIES ON RACE AND ETHNIC RELATIONS

Series Editor:

JOHN H. STANFIELD II

College of William and Mary

This series is designed for scholars working in creative theoretical areas related to race and ethnic relations. The series will publish books and collections of original articles that critically assess and expand upon race and ethnic relations issues from American and comparative points of view.

SERIES EDITORIAL BOARD

Volumes in this series include

1. Roger Waldinger, Howard Aldrich, Robin Ward, and Associates, ETHNIC ENTREPRENEURS: Immigrant Business in Industrial Societies
2. Philomena Essed, UNDERSTANDING EVERYDAY RACISM: An Interdisciplinary Theory
3. Samuel V. Duh, BLACKS AND AIDS: Causes and Origins
4. Steven J. Gold, REFUGEE COMMUNITIES: A Comparative Field Study
5. Mary E. Andereck, ETHNIC AWARENESS AND THE SCHOOL: An Ethnographic Study
6. Teun A. van Dijk, ELITE DISCOURSE AND RACISM
7. Rebecca Morales and Frank Bonilla, LATINOS IN A CHANGING U.S. ECONOMY: Comparative Perspectives on Growing Inequality
8. Gerhard Schutte, WHAT RACISTS BELIEVE: Race Relations in South Africa and the United States
9. Stephen Burman, THE BLACK PROGRESS QUESTION: Explaining the African American Predicament
10. Bette J. Dickerson, AFRICAN AMERICAN SINGLE MOTHERS: Understanding Their Lives and Families
11. Davia Stasiulis and Nira Yuval-Davis, UNSETTLING SETTLER SOCIETIES: Articulations of Gender, Race, Ethnicity and Class
12. Robyn M. Holmes, HOW YOUNG CHILDREN PERCEIVE RACE

How Young Children Perceive Race

Robyn M. Holmes

Sage Series on Race and Ethnic Relations

volume 12

SAGE Publications
International Educational and Professional Publisher
Thousand Oaks London New Delhi

For information address:

SAGE Publications, Inc.
2455 Teller Road
Thousand Oaks, California 91320

SAGE Publications Ltd.
6 Bonhill Street
London EC2A 4PU
United Kingdom

SAGE Publications India Pvt. Ltd.
M-32 Market
Greater Kailash I
New Delhi 110048 India

Printed in the United States of America

Library of Congress Cataloging-in-Publication Data

Holmes, Robyn M.
How young children perceive race / author, Robyn M. Holmes.
p. cm.—(Sage series on race and ethnic relations: 12)
Includes bibliographical references (p.) and indexes.
ISBN 0-8039-7108-7 (cl).—ISBN 0-8039-7109-5 (pb)
1. Race awareness in children. 2. Ethnicity in children.
3. Prejudices in children. I. Title. II. Series: Sage series on race and ethnic relations: v. 12.
BF723.R3H65 1995
155.4'18—dc20 94-23538

95 96 97 98 10 9 8 7 6 5 4 3 2 1

Sage Typesetter: Danielle Dillahunt

For Brian, Melissa, Brian Patrick, and Kevin

Contents

Series Editor's Introduction ix
John H. Stanfield II

Acknowledgments xi

1. Introduction 1

2. Field Methods: Working With Children 7
   - Selecting a Site 7
   - Contact With the Group 9
   - My Relationship With the Children 10
   - Research Methods, Data Collection, Field Notes, and Analyses 12
   - The Children 15
   - Problems and Solutions 17

3. The Elementary Schools 20
   - School Sites 20
   - General School Statistics 21
   - School Culture and Racial Integration 24
   - The Classrooms 27
   - Kindergarten 31

4. Categories and Cognition 34
   - The Principle of Dualism 34
   - The Children's Classification Scheme for People 40

5. Conceptions of Self 47
Self-Portraits and Conceptions of Self 48
The Children's Conceptions of Others 58

6. Friendship and Ethnicity 66
Cognitive Notions of Friendship 66
Organizing Principles 67
Taxonomy of Friend Terms 69
Categories of Friends 70
Ranking 72
The Children's Use of Friend Terms 73
The Rules of Friendship 74
Racial Relationships: Making a Friend 75
Friend Selection 78
The Girlfriend-Boyfriend Relationship 81

7. Procreation and Race 87
Childbirth and Procreation 88
Mommy and the Color of the Baby 93
The Children's Subjective Feelings on Interracial Unions 101

8. Conclusion 105

Appendix: Sample Tape Transcription 111

References 115

Author Index 127

Subject Index 131

About the Author 133

Series Editor's Introduction

This book is a wonderful ethnographic study of the attitudes and beliefs that young school children have about race and race relations. Robyn Holmes is representative of a growing number of scholars exploring the ways children learn "race" as a basis of social differentiation in their daily lives. The book also conveys much about the ways parents and other significant others, such as teachers, influence children's thinking about race and cross-racial bonding. In presenting her findings, Holmes reminds us that race is a social construction learned during young, tender ages and thus is not just an "adult" problem or issue.

John H. Stanfield II
Series Editor

Acknowledgments

For my doctoral dissertation, I conducted research on children's play and friendship. During that period of participant observation, many facets of children's social cognition emerged, particularly their racial beliefs. The children's candid conversations on such topics as interracial friendships and the influence of race on their selection of a "romantic" partner were quite revealing, and I soon found myself very attracted to this topic of inquiry. For the past 9 years, I have been interested primarily in children's perceptions of race and play behavior.

I thank Mitch Allen, Executive Editor; John H. Stanfield II, Series Editor; Diana E. Axelsen, Production Editor; Gillian Dickens, Editorial Assistant; Linda Poderski, Copy Editor; and Frances Borghi at Sage Publications for making the publication experience a very pleasant one.

Other individuals also have provided me with invaluable assistance. I thank warmly my colleagues at Monmouth College in New Jersey for their guidance and support: Janet Ward Schofield; Charles Kimble; and Anne Marie Pfaff, for designing Figures 3.1 and 3.2. I owe a special debt of gratitude to Brian Sutton-Smith for showing me the way around a playground and, ultimately, the classroom.

I lovingly thank my husband, Richard, for making life wonderful. I thank my sister and brother for letting me share in their children's lives. And I thank my parents for giving me their continued support and encouragement.

Finally, I thank all of the children who participated in this study. They graciously let me enter the world of childhood, and it was a journey that shall remain forever in my heart.

Robyn Holmes
New Jersey

1

Introduction

In her germinal work, Mary Ellen Goodman (1952) introduced to the scientific community ways to explore social concepts in young children and inspired other researchers to investigate the topics of race and ethnicity in young subjects. Since that work, much literature has been produced on these and related topics.

For example, numerous studies have explored racial preferences in young children (e.g., Aboud, 1977; Asher & Allen, 1969; Morland & Hwang, 1981; Singleton & Asher, 1979). These kinds of experimental studies typically employ contrived research designs. Such works attempt to elicit children's playmate preferences through the presentation of differently colored dolls, sociometric questionnaires, and the recording of interaction frequencies among children of differing races. In not one of these studies are conclusions drawn from the spontaneous and natural behavior of children. Rather, the above studies take as their goal narrowly defined research queries.

Other studies have concentrated on ethnic and self-identification abilities in young children. Such studies seek to determine how children define themselves and construct their sense of self (e.g., Aboud, 1987; Harter, 1988; Morland, 1966; Rosenberg, 1979; Semaj, 1980; Spencer, 1988; Williams & Morland, 1976). For the most part, these studies seek to discover how children acquire an ethnic identity and distinguish themselves from other children. Nevertheless, such works often rely on collecting children's responses to leading queries, such as, "Could a black person become a white person if . . . ?"

Results of such studies are presented as statistical tallies and are problematic for several reasons. First, it is possible that such queries do not measure accurately the children's perceptions or knowledge. Second, not measure accurately the children's perceptions or knowledge. Second, such queries necessarily lead to a yes or no response from a child without considering the child's thinking or reasoning processes. Third, researchers control the way they phrase a query for the children (e.g., Bierman & Schwartz, 1986; Parker, 1984). It seems reasonable to compare the way one poses a question to a child with the way courtroom attorneys can lead a witness to answer in predictable ways (e.g., Loftus, 1975).

Other kinds of works have concentrated on children's racial preferences in their social relationships. Asher, Singleton, and Taylor's (1982) study collected best friend nominations in a desegregated school. Whitley, Schofield, and Snyder's (1984) work focused on the criterion of mutual liking to examine friendships in a desegregated school. The latter work is a more recent version of earlier studies that collected ratings of liking for African American and European American children in an elementary school setting (e.g., Schofield & Francis, 1982; St. John & Lewis, 1975).

Conclusions drawn from these kinds of studies are also problematic and incomplete because they fail to account for the richness of human behavior that occurs among individuals, the nonverbal communication, and the social categories that are relevant to the children. Also implicit in the design of surveys is the difficulty in testing the validity of the responses unless they are verified by observations.

Finally, some studies have investigated prejudice in children. For example, Clark's (1966) work makes explicit use of presenting children with differently colored dolls to measure prejudice. The Clark Doll Test (CDT) was developed for African American children by Clark and Clark (1947) and used to measure the effects of societal devaluation on the children as a consequence of their racial group membership. Children were presented with two brown and two white dolls and were asked seven forced-choice questions, such as, "Which doll would you rather play with?" to assess the children's racial preferences and racial and self-identification abilities (see also Branch & Newcombe, 1986).

The more recent work of Aboud (1988) makes use of a Piagetian framework to explain the development of prejudice in children. Although Aboud's work claims to be a "child-oriented view," the practice of placing children's knowledge or behavior into age-related categories is contradictory to that goal. In this particular case, one categorizes a child by comparative terminology devised by the investigator and ignores what is relevant to the child in social encounters.

Although existing studies have contributed greatly to our understanding of race and ethnicity in children, current research endeavors need to take a different theoretical and methodological approach. If we are, as Clark (1966) suggested, a "child-centered society," then our existing research methods have failed to represent accurately children's perceptions of race and ethnicity and how these concepts affect their behavior.

Consider the recent inclination of researchers in various disciplines to take into account the child's point of view, rather than to rely on adult interpretations of children's activities (e.g., Chick, 1989; Corsaro, 1985; Fine, 1987; Holmes, 1991a, 1992b; Kelly-Byrne, 1989; King, 1987; Mandell, 1988). Such a perspective could be viable also for the study of race and ethnicity in children. As Aboud (1988) suggested, researchers need to examine interpersonal relationships and friendships to compile an accurate database of young children's knowledge of racial and ethnic concepts.

The intention of my work is to convey young children's knowledge of race and ethnicity in their own terms and to examine how this knowledge affects their social relationships and notions about procreation. The discussion below addresses methodological issues.

In contrast to the experimental studies mentioned above, my work employed the following methods of data collection: (a) participant observation (e.g., see Agar, 1980; Berentzen, 1989; Fine & Sandstrom, 1988; Spradley, 1980); (b) informal conversations; and (c) collection of the children's artwork (e.g., Coles, 1964).

During the entire period of research, I attended kindergarten in various schools and participated in all of the children's daily activities. Thus I learned to see the world through a child's eyes, rather than through those of an adult who simply observes and records children's behavior (e.g., Berentzen, 1989; Corsaro, 1985; Fine & Sandstrom, 1988; Holmes, 1991a; Kelly-Byrne, 1989). To this end, contrived experiments were employed sparingly, and the use of statistics was minimal, with the exception of those that give population or group characteristics.

In addition, the children were never interviewed in a formal fashion. Formality surely would have reinforced their notions of adult authority (e.g., Fine, 1987; Fine & Sandstrom, 1988; Mandell, 1988). Rather, the children were asked to draw an activity that children appear to engage in willingly (e.g., Gardner, 1980; Goodnow, 1977; Kellogg, 1969; Thomas & Silk, 1990).

Thus this book stands in contrast to Coles's (1964) seminal series *Children of Crisis,* which evaluated children's drawings for their psychological content. In my work, children's artwork is viewed as a medium through which children can express themselves on subjects they have difficulty in conveying verbally to adults (e.g., Freeman, 1987; Holmes, 1992a). Drawing tasks allowed me to converse informally with the children and provided them with the opportunity to express openly their notions of race and ethnicity.

Before proceeding with the general plan of the book, I present the reader with several definitions that appear throughout the text. Anthropologists have long debated the definition of *culture.* Numerous definitions exist in the literature, and one's choice is often a reflection of one's theoretical stance and research intentions. In this work, I share the view of culture advanced by Ward Goodenough (1957). For him, *culture* refers to a system of knowledge and ideational codes shared collectively by members of a group that guides behavioral outcomes. To quote Goodenough (1957, p. 167):

> A society's culture consists of whatever it is one has to know or believe in order to operate in a manner acceptable to its members. Culture is not a material phenomenon; it does not consist of things, people, behavior, or emotions. It is rather an organization of these things. It is the form of things that people have in their mind, their models for perceiving, relating, and otherwise interpreting them.

The same argument can be made for the term *race.* Some researchers view race as a biological construct useful for defining and categorizing populations of a species on the basis of differing gene frequencies (Buettner-Janusch, 1966). Other researchers view race as an arbitrary social and cultural construct useful for categorizing and distinguishing one group from another on the basis of some criterion—for example, skin color, language, or customary behavior.

Because of the arbitrary and imprecise nature of the existing biological and cultural definitions of race (Williams & Morland, 1976), I have abandoned this concept; it appears to have no utility. Rather, I have elected to focus on the "ethnic" group. Hence the distinctions made by Barth (1969, 1992) are relevant. In the text, *ethnic group* refers to those individuals who share and identify themselves as members of one group and who participate in a common cultural value system.

By contrast, *ethnic identity* is used in a more specific sense to indicate a person's ability to categorize himself or herself as a member of a particular ethnic group. For example, the information contained in the statement "I am Italian" conveys one's ethnic identity (e.g., Phinney, 1989; Phinney & Rotheram, 1987; Thompson, 1989) and the knowledge that one possesses the attributes common to that group (Aboud, 1988). This definition was expanded by Royce (1982) to include the adoption of feelings and behaviors by group members about the values and history that identify them as a group. As Roosens (1989) suggested, the latter term is viewed as a relational construct linked with the existence of the ethnic group.

Finally, it should be stated clearly that these terms are constructs devised by scholars and researchers and were never once uttered by the children.[1] Any phrase or verbal material taken directly from the children is enclosed in double quotation marks. Single quotation marks are used to denote a gloss of the children's terms. When a child's pseudonym appears in the text, it is followed by his or her fictional school affiliation in parentheses. This graphic convention gives the reader a sense of where the data were obtained.

In the following chapters, the reader discovers how children's conceptions of race and ethnicity affect their social behavior and notions of procreation. Chapter 2 contains information on the setting and an overview of the methods used during the research. Particular problems that must be confronted and resolved when working with children are discussed in detail. Also included are character descriptions of some of the children who were gracious enough to teach me over the years. These descriptions are included for two reasons: (a) It is often customary in ethnographic works for the investigator to include descriptions of informants (e.g., Chagnon, 1977), and (b) they give the reader images of the 5-year-olds who participated in the project. Chapter 3 contains information on the schools that were visited during the course of the research, on the classroom arrangements, and on the curricula.

In Chapter 4, the children's view of their universe is presented in the form of dualistic constructs. These are antithetical pairs, such as boy/girl and big/little, that the children employ to organize their world. For them, membership in one category of the pair is absolute in that it precludes membership in the other category of the pair. In addition, their knowledge of ethnicity and ability to categorize individuals into groups is discussed. On the basis of Piagetian frameworks, it is often presumed that young children are not capable of subsuming smaller categories into larger ones. This belief recently has been challenged (e.g., Holmes, 1991a; Mandler, 1990), and the children's ability to classify individuals into groups supports the contention that young children are indeed capable of these cognitive tasks. Aspects of categorization that emerge include the use of attributes and the notion of a focal type (e.g., Rosch, 1973; Rosch & Lloyd, 1978).

Chapter 5 presents a discussion of how the children view themselves. This includes their developing conceptions of self and ethnic identity. The text is complemented by self-portraits. Chapter 6 contains a discussion of the relationship between friendship and ethnicity. For these children, race is not a salient feature for determining friendship choices. Instead, it serves as a standard of comparison against the self. The same does not hold true in some cases for 'romantic' relationships. The children apply their notions of race to interracial romantic relationships, and race does appear to be a variable that affects the children's selection processes for potential partners. Chapter 7 contains the children's notions of procreation. These children are quite curious about bodily functions, anatomical differences between boys and girls, and prenatal development. Skin color plays an important role in their conceptions of procreation and parent-child resemblance. Finally, Chapter 8 presents conclusions based on the findings of the research and offers suggestions for future research. In the next chapter, the reader becomes acquainted with the task of conducting research with young children.

NOTE

1. The children do not use the terms *European American, African American,* and *Latino.* These are abstract, social constructs employed by the researcher to distinguish the children's different racial and ethnic groupings. These terms were difficult for most, if not all, of the children to comprehend. Rather, as revealed in Chapter 4, the children categorized people on the basis of superficial characteristics—for example, skin color. Hence, the words *brown, white,* and *black* appear throughout the text. Although I prefer not to use color terms to describe and classify people into groups, I employed the children's terms when speaking with the children.

2

Field Methods: Working With Children

Children rarely have the opportunity to express themselves orally in the presence of adults, and all too often children are admonished for intruding on adult conversations. Nevertheless, if we as researchers wish to develop viable education strategies, reform curricula to include a multicultural perspective, and foster interactions among students of differing ethnic backgrounds, then it is the children to whom we should be listening. Thus if the reader can discern the children's voices through the following pages of text, then I have accomplished much. This ethnographic work is an attempt to communicate racial and ethnic relationships through the eyes of a child.

SELECTING A SITE

Children spend approximately 15,000 hours of their lives at school (e.g., Rutter, Maugham, Mortimore, & Ouston, 1979), so I could think of no better place to visit with them regularly. Neighborhoods are also viable environments for observing children, but several limitations are associated with this territory. The first limitation pertains to the ethical concerns in dealing with children. Parental consent would have to be obtained for each child if interviews were employed. Otherwise, observations presumably would have to be collected outdoors in a covert manner. Thus it would be difficult to establish a relationship with the children as an adult stranger in a particular neighborhood. The second limitation pertains to the regularity of outdoor play. Climatic factors and parental permission would greatly affect the frequency of outdoor play. The third limitation pertains to the unlikelihood that a neighborhood contains a homogenous group of children with respect to age. In contrast, the classroom offers (a) regular access to a specific population of children, (b) an environment in which to observe the development of relationships among unfamiliar children, and (c) an opportunity for an investigator to interact and establish relationships with the children. Hence, the classroom provides an excellent atmosphere for viewing the formation and nurturance of racial relationships.

Kindergarten children were appealing for several reasons. First, school was usually their introductory experience in socialization with peers outside the security of the home and the neighborhood (with the exception of those children who previously had attended nursery school; e.g., Rizzo, 1989).

Second, early reconnaissance in the schools suggested that the kindergarten curriculum was more amenable to the goals of participant observation than the older grades were. The former's class schedule afforded the consummate environment for interacting with the children. Dispersed playtimes and special activities allowed me the freedom to wander about, play with the children, and hold conversations. By contrast, the rigid and traditional methods designed for the older grades confined these children to their stationary desks throughout most of the school day. Observation posed no problem, but participation was next to impossible. If in the end I wished to convey the children's perceptions, then participation was vital to gain a clear understanding of their world.

The third reason that weighed heavily in my decision was personal. I simply adore young children and have always enjoyed their company. As Johnson (1975) suggested, a researcher must feel comfortable with the group or community he or she wishes to study. I was especially comfortable interacting with children, unabashed by playing on the jungle gym with them during playtime and willing to listen to what they had to say (e.g., Fine & Sandstrom, 1988). I made the decision to conduct research with young children without hesitation. Indeed, a certain innocence, candor, and affection radiate from young children, and I am fascinated by the ease with which they speak the truth. Regrettably, these qualities often are lost in adulthood. Also, children say precisely what they mean even if it is not what you want to hear. Adults often tell you what they think you want to know and ought to hear.

CONTACT WITH THE GROUP

I approached the task of gaining access to the kindergarten children in a similar fashion for all of the schools. First, I contacted the school principals through telephone conversations, at which time I outlined briefly my research intentions. All of the principals found my proposal agreeable, and I was impresed by their graciousness. Their acceptance was only a tentative one and the first step in requesting admission to the kindergarten classes. Final approval for my project was obtained from the respective boards of education. This was accomplished by submitting explanatory letters that detailed the nature of the project, its goals, data collection methods, and a promise to protect the children's and the schools' anonymity.

Ethical concerns are an issue particularly when working with young children (e.g., Agar, 1980; Fine & Sandstrom, 1988; Langer, 1985), and this matter was discussed with each principal. All of the schools and the children who participated in the project were protected through the use of pseudonyms, and although photographs were taken of the children, none was ever used in any publication. In 1985, Corsaro conducted work with nursery school children and elected to view their personal school records. By contrast, the principals and I concurred that personal information from the children's school files be omitted because it was irrelevant to the project and because their rights as informants would be further protected.

I also requested that my introduction to the children inform them briefly of my research intentions. This is what Fine and Sandstrom (1988) defined as "shallow cover" for the investigator; it is discussed in detail later in this chapter. The principals left to my discretion the formality of my introduction to the children, and it was performed by the children's teachers. Finally, the principals granted my request to use a tape recorder.

After approval from the boards of education, I met again with each principal and the host kindergarten teacher. During our second conversation, the principals and I discussed my visitation privileges. These ranged from one day to several days per week, and the kindergarten teachers were especially accommodating with scheduling my visits to their classes. In every school, the final decision of selecting a class was always left to me.

My recollection of the first kindergarten I visited for the project is still very graphic. The first thing I noticed was the toy collection. It decorated the perimeter of the room. Miniature tables and chairs filled the center.

Everything looked so small! For the first time in years, fond memories of my own kindergarten resurfaced. Viewing each successive class for the first time affected me in some way, and I left each school feeling eager to meet the children.

Throughout the research, I became acquainted with numerous faculty and staff members. Everyone made me feel like a vital part of the school, rather than a meddling investigator. The kindergarten teachers made my task especially uncomplicated and were accommodating in every respect. From the very first day, I felt welcome in all of the classrooms. The teachers and I had frequent conversations throughout my stay at each school concerning the progress and findings of the research. Their comments were insightful, and their involvement was very much appreciated. They represented a perspective neither the children nor I could have supplied.

MY RELATIONSHIP WITH THE CHILDREN

A grown-up who simply shows up on the first day of class with a child's knapsack can neither expect the children to believe he or she is a new student nor make his or her adult status disappear (e.g., Agar, 1980; Mandell, 1988). Adult researchers must provide the children with some type of justification for their presence. This is what Fine (1980) termed a "researcher's cover."

The approach taken for this project was *shallow cover* as defined by Fine and Sandstrom (1988) and employed by Fine (1987) in his work with a Little League baseball team. Shallow cover provides the group being studied with a vague or partial explanation of the project but does not describe the project in detail (e.g., Llewellyn, 1980).

My introduction to the children was crucial. I did not want to foster an authoritarian teacher-student relationship. I wanted to gain their trust and become one of their classmates.

To my chagrin, in two of the schools (Lawrence and Joseph), the teachers introduced me as "Miss Holmes, who will be spending time with you to learn about friendship." I was uncomfortable with having the children address me by title and surname because this is the way the children address their teachers. Although I asked the children to call me by my first name, they still called me "Mrs. Holmes." To avoid a potential comparison with their teachers, I concentrated on behaving like a child, rather than as an adult.

In the other classes, I asked explicitly that the teachers introduce me by my first name to the children. Mrs. Baker (Concord) made the following statement to her class: "This is a new student, Robyn, who will be with us every Friday. Make her feel welcome and help her learn the class rules." I took my seat, where a box of crayons with my name on it was placed. In these classes, the children addressed me freely by my first name from the moment I was introduced to them. I found this strategy effective because it seemed to attenuate the children's notions of adult authority and to strengthen my position as one of their classmates. My authority was further weakened by the teachers who treated me like another student as much as possible. I was surprised by the children's early acceptance of me, and I asked for their assistance in framing questions and encouraged them to approach me during playtimes.

I suspect that, in the former case of my introduction to the children, they associated me with their teachers, the majority of whom were female and married (e.g., Everhart, 1983; Glassner, 1976). Nevertheless, the comparison ended here. I never once received the reference label "teacher," which some of the children used in requesting assistance. This label was reserved exclusively for teachers and was conferred on substitutes in their absence. In fact, I was often spoken of in direct contrast to their teachers, presumably because my behavior was often atypical. One day I was playing with a toy that, unbeknownst to me, was not available for the children at playtime. Eric (Thoreau) ran over from his playgroup to warn me, "Robyn, you're not supposed to play with this. Hurry and put it back before the teacher sees you."

My relationship with the children approximates the "friend role" described by Fine and Sandstrom (1988) and used by various researchers who work with young children (e.g., Corsaro, 1985; Fine, 1987; Holmes, 1991a, 1991b; Kelly-Byrne, 1989). I was always available to play with the children and rarely disciplined them unless the situation demanded adult intervention—for example, in cases of physical injury. My authority was, at best, dubious. Eventually, I earned their trust and became a worthy playmate. Sometimes the children indicated the special quality of our relationship and rewarded me with the label "best friend" (e.g., Corsaro, 1985; Fine & Sandstrom, 1988). Mickey (Thoreau) and I were walking in from outdoor play when he remarked, "Robyn, we had fun. You're my best friend." I was very taken by his statement and knew I was learning to see the world from a child's viewpoint. As Murphy (1985) suggested, children, even if provided with an explanation for an adult researcher's presence, make their own interpretations based on the adult's behavior.

RESEARCH METHODS, DATA COLLECTION, FIELD NOTES, AND ANALYSES

This book is, in part, a response to the need to present young children's conceptions of racial and ethnic knowledge from their perspective. Because a person's theoretical stance determines, in part, how he or she views a particular research endeavor and formulates conclusions based on the collected data, I present the approaches taken in this project.

First, I am guided by the anthropological theories and methods of Agar (1980), Dougherty (1985), Geertz (1973), Goodenough (1956), Spradley (1972, 1980), Turner and Bruner (1986), and Tyler (1969). Second, I view the children as members of an exotic culture (e.g., Goode, 1986; Speier, 1976) and take as my goal that commonly associated with cultural anthropologists: an ethnography that provides an accurate description of the children's knowledge and behavior in matters of race and ethnicity.

As an ethnographer, my goal is to provide detailed descriptions to convey the nuances of the children's behavior and the culturally relevant criteria by which they assign meaning to their own behavior (Goodenough, 1956). My aim is to find patterns in the children's thinking that lead to an analysis of their substance, rather than simply to account for them (Geertz, 1973). Such an approach allows me to move from simply recording behavior and conversations to interpret these experiences through subjective and personal feelings, expectations, and meaning (e.g., Turner & Bruner, 1986).

Method

Data were gathered primarily through participant observation (e.g., Agar, 1980; Berentzen, 1989; Corsaro, 1985; Fine & Sandstrom, 1988; Johnson, 1975; Spradley, 1980). Extensive observations were recorded during a 6-year period on school premises encompassing all of the daily activities of kindergarten children. In short, wherever the children went, I went with them (e.g., Holmes, 1991a, 1992b).

To supplement observations, I spoke with the children informally during playtime. Formal interviewing made the children far too uncomfortable, and it was almost impossible to interview one child at a time (e.g., Bierman & Schwartz, 1986; Parker, 1984). In addition, I wanted to remain as much like one of the children as possible. To this end, I simply talked with my classmates while we played because this is what the children usually do with their peers. This method was productive, and the children responded freely to all types of questions. They were fascinated by the tape recorder, which often attracted their attention. I was able to record categories of people, their attributes, and their conceptions of race, color, and interracial relationships. Such information was easy to elicit as the children and I played together.

The tape recorder did have its drawbacks, however. The background noise at playtime often made it necessary to make verbatim accounts of conversations to clarify tape transcriptions. This also sparked the children's curiosity because they could not understand my ability to write on endlessly.

It also occurred to me early on that the children loved to draw and did so voluntarily. They appeared to find immense enjoyment in the activity, and I began to wonder whether they might draw for me. Because the children conveyed their interpretations of the world in their artwork (e.g., Gardner, 1980; Goodnow, 1977; Kellogg, 1969; Thomas & Silk, 1990), self-portraits and portraits of friends and people from different ethnic groups contributed substantially to the study of the children's knowledge of racial relationships (e.g., Coles, 1964).

While they were drawing, I asked the children to describe their pictures for me. This not only revealed their conceptions of self and race but also gave me access to impressions and subjective feelings about specific individuals and relationships (e.g., Turner & Bruner, 1986). Drawings were not restricted to the subject matter of race and ethnicity, and I was quite surprised by the diversity of themes, as diverse as scribbles and marriage and God.

Finally, I brought a camera. It helped with my recollection of friend choices, playgroup compositions, and seating arrangements. Of course, I also could not resist immortalizing those little faces on film.

Data Collection

In all of the classes, I sat with the children either at their tables or in my own assigned seat. The teachers were especially accommodating in this respect and moved my location each week so that I had the opportunity to sit with all of the children.

My interactions with the children occurred during free-play periods, snacktime, and special activities (e.g., participation in physical education classes). At other times during the class day, I was engaged in activities that occurred at our seats—for example, worksheets and art projects. I let the children approach me when they were ready to do so and was pleased that their early reactions toward me were favorable. I encouraged them to approach me, and on their cue, we started discussing the subject of racial relationships.

Field Notes

Written notations were in the customary form of field notes. These contained condensed accounts of observations, class activities, verbatim phrases, and conversations. Divisions of the entries corresponded to school activities. Thus, if the children were in the gym, I wrote down the time, the activity, and subsequent observations.

I kept a notebook and tape recorder with me during playtime. This was the time of day when the children were invited either individually or as members of a group to sit and draw with me. (The group size never exceeded four children.) While they worked on their creations, I asked them questions about the pictures and matters pertaining to ethnicity. Almost all of our conversations were tape-recorded. At the end of the school day, all notes were transcribed into expanded accounts of the day's activities (Holmes, 1991a, 1992b).

Finally, all tapes were transcribed completely after each session (see the Appendix for a sample tape transcription). Because of the background noise on the tape, I found it wise to jot down important phrases while the children were speaking.

Analyses

Observations were analyzed by the method presented in Burling's (1969) article on ethnographic theory, which suggests that linguistic viewpoints and approaches (the task of writing grammatical descriptions) can be extended to provide ethnographic analysis of other aspects of culture. Taped transcriptions (casual speech and conversational material) were analyzed and coded for classificatory data, including categories of people, attributes and focal members of categories, and knowledge of procreation (e.g., Rosch, 1973; Rosch & Lloyd, 1978; Spradley, 1980).

THE CHILDREN

Between 1986 and 1992, I visited five kindergarten classes that had a combined enrollment of 102 children. The children's population statistics were (a) 54 girls and 48 boys, (b) 44 African American children, 42 European American children, 12 Latino children, and 4 children who belonged to other ethnic groups.

Although I draw freely from the observations and conversations with all of the children, my understanding of their knowledge of racial and ethnic relationships was communicated regularly to me by my informants and through observations and informal chats with the children. Nevertheless, some children and I became special classmates. Because it is often customary in ethnographic works to include descriptions of informants (e.g., Chagnon, 1977), I have done so. Some of my special classmates are described below.

Todd (Lawrence)

Todd has sandy blond hair and blue eyes. He is taller than his classmates and by virtue of his size might well be mistaken for an older child. He interacts easily with both boys and girls and is a popular choice by the children for desirable classroom duties, such as co-line leader. What stands out in my mind is the way he seriously contemplated my questions.

Sharon (Lawrence)

Sharon has sandy blond hair and brown eyes. She is relatively small in stature but full of vitality. She is talkative, bossy, and quite knowledgeable in social matters. She loves wearing sunglasses and hair bands as if she were a fashion designer setting a new trend. I was constantly amazed by our conversations and the ease with which she spoke of delicate matters. She was the only child who comfortably called me by my first name in a class where the other children addressed me as "Mrs. Holmes."

Jack (Bryant)

Jack is an adorable child. He has light brown skin, deep brown eyes, and a soft, whispery voice. He was the first child to approach me in his class, and from that moment on we became friends. He likes to play with the boys, draw, and play bingo.

Tess (Thoreau)

Tess has dark brown skin and dark brown eyes. She is probably one of the most sociable children I have ever met. She is full of vitality, has a contagious laugh, and would draw endlessly for me. She is well liked by her classmates and loves to play house.

Melissa (Concord)

Melissa has an olive complexion, long brown hair that is always pulled back, and brown eyes. She is an especially patient child for a 5-year-old. She has a gentle voice, is a great conversationalist, and loves to color with markers. Although she usually plays with the girls, she has a "best boy friend" in class.

Charley (Concord)

Charley has light blond hair and blue eyes. He is the tallest child in his class and, at times, uses his size to his advantage. Some of the children even have referred to him as a "bully." Nevertheless, he is an enigma. At times, he is cooperative and demonstrates leadership qualities; at other times, he is the antagonist. He is occasionally very affectionate with his classmates and plays exclusively with the boys.

Mickey (Thoreau)

Mickey has light brown skin and dark brown eyes. He is the smallest child in all of the classes but is especially energetic, even for a young child. I must have pushed him on the swings at least 1,000 times, and he laughed with delight as he soared higher with each push. He is a bit bashful, yet has several best friends in class. He tends to play mostly with the boys and favors the computer during playtime.

Garry (Joseph)

Garry has light blond hair and blue eyes. He is a particularly athletic child, strong and sturdy, who possesses a strong sense of self. He loves to play on the swings, and I never once passed on his request to push him "up to the sky."

Stefan (Bryant)

Stefan has dark brown skin, dark brown eyes, and short black hair. He is the king of gossip and was a direct source of information for me and his classmates. As soon as I entered the classroom, he would fill me in on who was "going with" whom and other delicious rumors. He loves to play with the blocks.

PROBLEMS AND SOLUTIONS

There is no denying that a field-worker experiences some difficulties in his or her attempt to gain insight into a child's world. The goal, however, is not an impossible one (e.g., Waksler, 1986). A researcher faces several inherent problems as a grown-up participating in the culture of childhood within the context of the school. The first problem is the matter of experimenter bias. Children are undeniably delightful creatures, and treating them objectively was a bit difficult. However, do not presume that I found all of these children to be perfectly wonderful. It was difficult to establish relationships with some of the shier children, and some children were, to say the least, annoying at times.

Nevertheless, certain children could always convince me to let them draw or stop what I was doing at the moment to join them. These children and I developed a special rapport. Although at times I did favor certain children with my attention, this never affected the results of the research or my ability to collect and analyze the data. If anything, these special relationships enabled me to gain a richer insight because the children trusted me (e.g., Corsaro, 1985; Fine & Sandstrom, 1988; Holmes, 1991a).

The second problem is that a researcher's presence will affect the children's behavior to some degree (e.g., Agar, 1980; Murphy, 1985). In my case, the teachers did their best to treat me like a "student," but my adult status was omnipresent. Sometimes I was a distraction in class. The children would call out my name when I entered the room or plead with me to sit at their table all while the teacher was trying to organize a class activity (the teachers were quite patient and never once mentioned that I was the cause of the children's outbursts).

The third problem is the difficulty in questioning the children (e.g., Bierman & Schwartz, 1986; Holmes, 1991a; Parker, 1984). How I phrased a question often determined the child's response. Thus when I asked, "Do you think there are different kinds of people?" I received answers pertaining to ethnicity. I received quite a different reply when I phrased the question, "What kind of person is a particular person?" Here, the children responded with attributes (e.g., Holmes, 1991a). I was conscious of how I framed a question so as not to lead the children into the desired response (e.g., see Loftus, 1975, and her work with eyewitness testimony). Thus I learned to phrase a question in several ways, and all of the children received a similar set of questions. I soon realized that open-ended questions led to the most detailed and productive types of responses.

The fourth problem is that collecting drawings from the children has its own set of difficulties. In my work, some of the children were often possessive of my attention and would think nothing of interrupting a drawing session to ask me to play with them. The teachers' assistance was welcome here, and the teachers often would direct the intruding child away from my table. I worked out an agreement with the children by giving each child "special time" to draw for me. This served to eliminate some of the interruptions that occurred during the tape-recorded drawing sessions.

On some occasions, a child would draw for me and describe the picture in detail before they actually began to draw for me. (All of the description was tape-recorded.) Then the child would ask to take the picture home to a parent or other relative. To prevent this from happening all the time, I used the following strategies: (a) I asked the children whether I could take the pictures home, and (b) if the children asked to take the pictures home, I asked them to draw for me first, and then I provided them with more materials for the drawing they wanted to take home.

The fifth problem is the domination at playtime reported by Kelly-Byrne (1989) in her play research with a young female child and the placing of the researcher in a compromising situation. I was lucky; I experienced no domination at playtime, nor did the children ever place me in a compromising situation. The latter was reported by adults working with somewhat older children (e.g., Best, 1983; Fine, 1987). At the very worst, the children would ask me to help them with their worksheets.

The final problem is that the topics of race and ethnicity are, regrettably, sensitive issues for some adults. For me, a major concern was whether my own ethnicity would affect the children's responses. During the course of the research, I experienced no difficulties in establishing relationships with the children, and none of the children refused to interact with me because of my ethnicity. Studies by Clark, Hocevar, and Dembo (1980), Corenblum and Wilson (1982), Gurkin (1968), Jones (1968), and Moore

(1976) also reported that the ethnicity of the examiner did not affect the children's ethnic attitudes.

Contrary to existing literature (Aboud, 1988; Clark, 1966; Cook, 1984; Katz & Taylor, 1988; Schofield, 1986), I found the children as a group to be relatively unprejudiced (Cook, 1985; Johnson & Johnson, 1981; Slavin, 1983). Nevertheless, I never naively presumed that my presence, ethnicity, and gender did not affect their behavior. The last, in fact, probably made my transition from grown-up to classmate easier because children are usually less fearful of female strangers than they are of male strangers (e.g., Lewis & Brooks-Gunn, 1972).

3

The Elementary Schools

SCHOOL SITES

Ethnographic data were collected from 1986 to 1992 at five elementary schools. I attended each school a minimum of one day per week for the entire academic year and also participated in special activities such as Halloween parties and class trips. This visitation schedule yielded approximately 60 sessions with each kindergarten class, equivalent to 150 hours of observation. All of the schools were located in a northeastern state, and a further demographic division placed them in either a city or township of the same county. Census statistics for the respective school locales are as follows:

The City of Walden

In 1990, a population of 16,799 resided in 6,871 households in the city of Walden. Approximately 55% of the population was between the ages of 18 and 65, with a median age of 32.6. Of the total population, approximately 59% was African American, 35% was European American, and 9% was Latino. The mean family income was $18,934 (U.S. Bureau of the Census, 1990).

Richard Township

In 1990, Richard Township's population of 28,148 resided in 10,395 households. Approximately 58% of the population was between the ages of 18 and 65, with a median age of 34.5. Of the total population, approximately 63% was European American, 34% was African American, and 4% was Latino. The median family income was $22,479 (U.S. Bureau of the Census, 1990).

Frost Township

In 1990, Frost Township's population of 25,058 resided in 9,261 households. Approximately 59% of the population was between the ages of 18 and 65, with a median age of 33.8. Of the total population, approximately 90% was European American, 5% was African American, and 3% was Latino. The median family income was $32,048 (U.S. Bureau of the Census, 1990).

The City of Limmerick

In 1990, Limmerick's population of 28,658 resided in 11,544 households. Approximately 60% of the population was between the ages of 18 and 65, with a median age of 34.7. Of the total population, approximately 57% was African American, 36% was European American, and 7% was Latino. The mean family income was $26,302 (U.S. Bureau of the Census, 1990).

GENERAL SCHOOL STATISTICS

Bryant Elementary School

Bryant Elementary School (Grades K-3) is located in the city of Walden and is one of three elementary schools that service the area. The city also has one intermediate school (Grades 4-6), one middle school (Grades 7-8), and one high school.

Bryant School is located in the southwest region of the city in a residential area. The school is only a few years old and stands adjacent to its predecessor. The school's interior is especially bright and cheery and symmetrical in design, and the corridors and classrooms are spacious. The kindergarten classrooms are located at the end of the east wing, on the first floor.

The school had a total enrollment of 411 students, and this population was approximately 75% African American, 17% Latino, and 8% European

American.[1] All of the children either walked to school or were transported by car. In contrast to the student body, the faculty (34 members) was approximately 58% European American and 42% African American. The majority were female and married. The school had one administrator—a principal—responsible for all of the duties concerning the functioning of the school. In addition, the school had several full-time teacher's aides, a custodial staff, and several administrative assistants.

Concord Elementary School

Concord Elementary School (Grades K-6) is located in Richard Township and is one of three elementary schools, along with one junior high school and one high school, that service the area. Concord Elementary School is located in the south central portion of the township on a residential street. It is a modern structure with a spacious playground and an abundance of outdoor play equipment. The kindergarten classrooms are located on the first floor at the end of the east and west hallways.

The school population was approximately 55% European American, 45% African American, and 5% Latino. The school had a total enrollment of 325 students, and approximately 75% of the children were bused to school. The faculty was approximately 69% European American and 31% African American, with two Latino faculty members. In addition, one administrator—the principal—managed the functioning of the school. Teaching duties were divided among 26 faculty members—23 female and 3 male. The majority of the females were married. Finally, the school had a full-time staff of eight employees, including an administrative assistant, a nurse, and a librarian.

Lawrence Elementary School

Lawrence Elementary School (Grades K-4) is located in Frost Township and is one of three elementary schools that service the district. There is also one intermediate school (Grades 5-8) and one high school. Lawrence Elementary School is located on the southeastern border of the township on a residential block. It is an older structure and has an old schoolhouse charm. The kindergarten classrooms are located on the first floor at the ends of the east and west wings.

The school population was approximately 95% European American, with the remaining 5% comprising all other ethnic groups. The school had a total enrollment of 410 students, and approximately 90% of the children came to school by bus. The remaining 10% resided within walking distance of the school. The faculty and staff were European American, and the principal was the sole administrator. Teaching duties were divided among 35 faculty members—32 female and 3 male. The majority of the females were married. In addition, the school had a full-time staff of eight employees, including an administrative assistant, a nurse, a librarian, and a custodial crew.

Thoreau Elementary School

Thoreau Elementary School (Grades K-8) is located in the city of Limmerick and is one of three elementary schools, along with one high school, that service the city. Thoreau Elementary School is located in the center of the city on a residential street. It is an older building with no playground. Recess takes place on streets that are barricaded by sawhorses and guarded by playground supervisors while the children are engaged in outdoor play. The kindergarten classrooms are located on the first floor at the rear of the building.

The school population was approximately 60% African American, 30% European American, and 10% Latino. The school had a total enrollment of 385 students, and approximately 95% of the children resided within walking distance of the school. The faculty was approximately 60% European American and 40% African American. One faculty member was Latino. In addition, one administrator—a principal—managed the functioning of the school. Teaching duties were divided among 29 faculty members—24 female and 5 male. The majority of the females were married. In addition, the school had a full-time staff of six employees, including an administrative assistant, a nurse, a librarian, and a cafeteria crew.

Joseph Elementary School

Joseph Elementary School (Grades K-8) is also located in Limmerick and is one of three elementary schools, along with one high school, that service the city. Joseph Elementary School is located in the northeast corner of the city on a residential street. The kindergarten classrooms are located on the first floor at the ends of the north and south corridors.

The school population was approximately 45% African American, 35% European American, and 20% Latino. The school had a total enrollment of 311 students, and approximately 95% of the children resided within walking distance of the school. The faculty was approximately 69% European American and 31% African American; five faculty members were Latino. One administrator—the principal—managed the functioning of the school. Teaching duties were divided among 27 faculty members—25 female and 2 male. The majority of the females were married. In addition, the school had a full-time staff of seven employees, including an administrative assistant, a nurse, a librarian, and a custodial crew.

SCHOOL CULTURE AND RACIAL INTEGRATION

Although the institutions that participated in this project were all elementary schools, salient differences were found between them. First was the issue of school locale. Parents today are concerned, and rightfully so, with their children's safety. Concord, Joseph, and Lawrence Schools were located in relatively crime-free neighborhoods, and most children either walked to school or came by bus. Some young children even walked to school unescorted. By contrast, Bryant and Thoreau Schools were located in neighborhoods where buildings were covered with graffiti and the crime rate was high. In these schools, parents, adult caretakers, and older siblings escorted the kindergarten children who resided within walking distance. When Kristin's (Thoreau) mother (a single parent) was ill, I walked Kristin home to ensure her safety.

Second was the matter of social demographics. Based on teacher reports and conversations with the children, the following statements reflect household composition for the participating schools:

- The highest percentage of children who come from single parent households (with the mother as head of the household) attend Thoreau School. In decreasing order, single-parent families are found in Joseph, Bryant, Concord, and Lawrence Schools.
- The highest percentage of children from divorced households attend Concord School. In decreasing order, children of divorce are found in Lawrence, Bryant, Joseph, and Thoreau Schools.
- The highest percentage of children born to interracial couples attend Bryant School, and the highest percentage of children born to interethnic parents attend Concord School.

Third was the issue of racial and ethnic variability among the schools' student populations. Bryant, Joseph, and Thoreau Schools had a racial majority of African American children; Lawrence School had a racial majority of European American children; and Concord School had an almost equal majority of African American and European American children.

Despite the differences in social demographics and the racial variability within and among the classes, the tone and atmosphere of each kindergarten class were similar. Most of the children arrived at school with knapsacks and enjoyed socializing with their classmates on entering class. The first few minutes of each class were spent in either free play or conversation. Common topics were movies, television shows, anecdotes from playing at each other's houses, and boyfriends and girlfriends. All of the children appeared to enjoy the same kinds of activities, perhaps because of their membership in the culture of 5-year-olds (Corsaro & Eder, 1990).

I never once in any school witnessed an interracial or intraracial physical confrontation among kindergarten children, although a teacher from Thoreau School informed me of two interracial incidents involving the same two boys from a higher grade. Because all of the kindergartens had a similar tone and culture, I discuss collectively the following topics on the children's racial beliefs and attitudes.

In 1985, Hallinan and Smith reported that prejudice was reduced in classes that were racially balanced and tended to increase when a racial majority was present. Given the different proportions of races in each class, one would expect to find some prejudiced attitudes in these schools. However, racial harmony was observed in all of the classrooms regardless of the racial and ethnic student percentages. How, then, is the observed racial harmony among these kindergarten children in schools with diverse racial compositions explained even though it contradicts the racial tensions researchers have found in a large number of schools (Gerard, 1983; Gerard & Miller, 1975; Hawley, 1988; Katz & Taylor, 1988; St. John, 1975; Worchel, 1986)?

As Cook (1984) suggested, perhaps the contrasting results were due to the conditions and contexts in which the various studies were conducted. A more critical answer, I think, lies in the interaction between two factors common to the kindergarten experience.

First is the question of whether racial integration in schools has been effective (Cook, 1984, 1985; Gerard, 1983; Katz & Taylor, 1988; Worchel, 1986). Apparently, contact in itself is not sufficient to reduce prejudice, for if this were true, school desegregation should have been successful

(Cook, 1984). Research evidence has demonstrated that desegregation has not facilitated the breaking down of racial barriers (Gerard, 1983; Katz & Taylor, 1988; Schofield, 1979, 1986; Stephan, 1978).

However, a majority of these cited studies were conducted in middle schools with older children. The racial and gender cleavage that surfaces in the latter elementary school years (Hallinan & Teixeira, 1987; Maccoby, 1990; Schofield, 1984) was not observed in any measurable frequency for the kindergarten children in my project. Thus a child's age and cognitive abilities may be one factor that could account for the racial harmony observed.

For example, because of a lack of cognitive maturity, young children tend to identify and focus on superficial characteristics and differences among people (Aboud, 1988; Butler, 1989; Harter, 1983; Ramsey, 1987). They are not yet capable of making psychological distinctions between ingroup and outgroup members, succumbing to peer pressure that discourages interracial friendships, and recognizing the importance of similar mores and attitudes as a basis for interpersonal attraction and friendship (Caspi & Herbener, 1990; Feingold, 1988; Hallinan & Teixeira, 1987; Maccoby, 1990; Maccoby & Jacklin, 1987; Magaro & Ashbrook, 1985; Schofield, 1984). It is possible that these factors also may be responsible for the racial and gender prejudices observed in the latter elementary grades.

Second is the influence of a school's curriculum on the effectiveness of racial integration. The more rigid, traditional curriculum of the latter elementary grades provides little opportunity for small cooperative group projects. Rather, students are confined to their seats for most of the school day, and their voluntary and cooperative interactions with peers are restricted to recess periods. As Aronson (1986), Cook (1984), and Worchel (1986) suggested, the failure to create cooperative, pleasant interactions in schools has hindered the development of interracial relations. Herein lies the strength of the kindergarten curriculum in improving race relations.

It has been demonstrated that the use of interracial cooperative groups in schools produces positive effects on interracial attitudes and race relations (Cook, 1985; Goleman, 1989; Hollifield & Slavin, 1983; Johnson & Johnson, 1981; Minuchin & Shapiro, 1983; Singh, 1991; Slavin, 1986, 1990). It seems possible that the racial harmony observed with the kindergarten children of this study could be due, in part, to the format of the curriculum that provides positive experiences with racial outgroup members through voluntary cooperative small group projects.

Thus it is my contention that the lack of racial tensions among these kindergarten children from racially diverse schools was facilitated by two interactive factors: (a) the age and cognitive abilities of the children studied and (b) a school curriculum that provided ample opportunities for small cooperative group interactions leading to early positive experiences with racial outgroup members.

THE CLASSROOMS

In every elementary school, the kindergarten classrooms were located on the first floor at the end of a corridor or wing. This physical isolation from the higher grades is a reflection of the ambivalent position of kindergarten as a transitional school grade that lacks a strong affiliation to either early childhood or elementary education curricula (e.g., Caldwell, 1989; Granucci, 1990).

Although the areas in which the schools were located varied by degree of ethnic population percentages and socioeconomic levels, all of the kindergarten classrooms had similar physical arrangements, learning materials, and toy selections. The teacher's desk was the focal point of every room, although it was used by all of the teachers as a storage shelf, rather than as a central area from which they taught. Rooms were decorated to the teachers' personal tastes, and among items displayed were alphabet letters and the children's handiwork.

School toys were kept on the perimeter of the rooms and stored in either bins or shelves. Each classroom had a play corner for "house," blocks, art table, painting easel, learning toys, and computer. Sample kindergarten classrooms from Lawrence and Bryant Schools appear in Figures 3.1 and 3.2, respectively.

Although the classrooms had similar materials and were often spatially analogous, they had different seating arrangements that created disparate social environments. The children in the classroom shown in Figure 3.1 were arranged in horizontal rows that in reality were either individual desks or tables placed in juxtaposition. Seating was preassigned by the teacher, and a child's seat was permanent unless his or her disruptive behavior necessitated relocation. In most cases, the emergent pattern was boy-girl-boy-girl.

Interaction for these children during class was limited to those sitting in close proximity (Gump, 1978; Rizzo, 1989). The alternate boy-girl scheme, however, was conducive to the formation and maintenance of

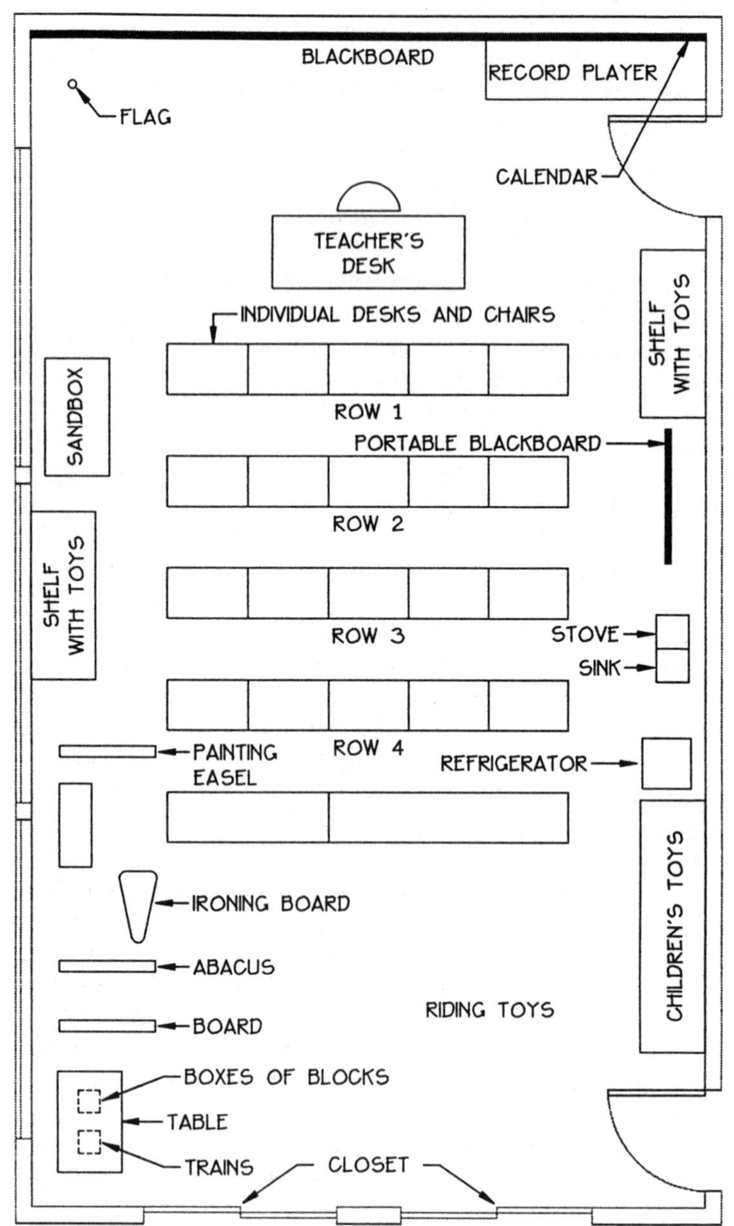

Figure 3.1. Classroom with horizontal rows of seats.

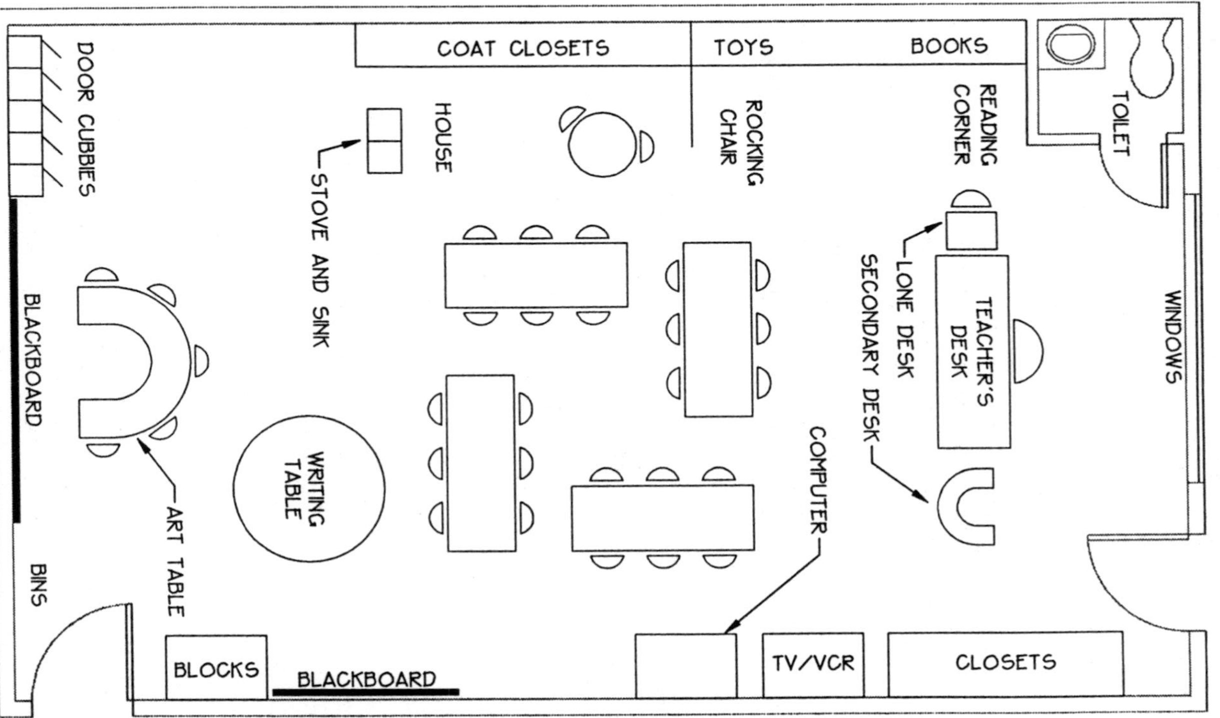

 Figure 3.2. Classroom with individual tables and chairs.

both same-sex and cross-sex dyad or pair relationships. Classes with this arrangement had a proportionately higher incidence of friendship of the latter kind, in comparison with that of the seating arrangements found in other classes.

By contrast, the seating of the room shown in Figure 3.2 was arranged in four individual tables with six chairs at each table. In classes with this arrangement, seat selection was assigned by the teacher or was a child's personal choice. In the latter case, a greater preference for same-sex tables and playgroups consequently developed. These kinds of seating arrangements did not facilitate the development of pair or dyad friendship types found in the horizontal row arrangement. Rather, children who sat together at a table later played with their tablemates and "friends" in groups.

Particular classroom seating arrangements appeared to facilitate the development of interracial and ethnic social relationships. The examples below illustrate the influence that classroom seating patterns had on the children's friendships.

> Wendy (Bryant) was one of three European American females in her class. She sat at a table with five African American children. This table often played "house" as a group, and Wendy was a welcome and obliging playmate. Although she had other "friends" in class, her friend ties to the classmates at her table were the strongest. Because children who sat together at a table eventually became playmates, Wendy was able to develop and maintain friendships with children she might not have chosen as friends if she were seated at a different table (e.g., Epstein & Karweit, 1983; Rizzo, 1989).

Numerous researchers (Aboud, 1988; Cook, 1985; Goleman, 1989; Minuchin & Shapiro, 1983; Singh, 1991; Slavin, 1986, 1990) reported that small cooperative group projects improve interracial relations, and the children's playgroups formed on the basis of table membership are an example of a cooperative group project (Bretherton, 1984). Wendy's interracial friendships were a direct result of positive small group experiences and the classroom seating pattern.

> Rich (Concord), an African American boy, was given a new seat at a table with four European American children. After increased interaction and positive play experiences with these children, Rich began to refer openly to his new tablemates as "friends." Once formed, the children's friendship ties remained intact throughout the school year.

In this second example, seating was preassigned by the teacher but was changed intentionally and periodically by her throughout the year to give the children new social experiences. Within a few weeks, the new seating pattern affected the children's verbal and behavioral friendship choices. Such observations are supported by research that contends that both interracial and intraracial children's friendships are stable relationships maintained during the school year (Berndt & Hoyle, 1985; Hallinan & Williams, 1987; Holmes, 1990).

Such examples support the social psychological literature (Arkin & Burger, 1980; Hays, 1985; Newcomb, 1981; Priest & Sawyer, 1967) that suggests geographic nearness is a prerequisite and powerful determinant of friendship formation. Proximity also promotes liking by increasing the number of chances children have to discover what they have in common (Newcomb, 1981; Saegert, Swap, & Zajonc, 1973; Zajonc, 1968).

The notion that proximity facilitates the development of friendships, conjoined with Pettigrew's (1986) suggestion that exposure is often effective in reducing prejudice if it brings about interpersonal contact, is essential knowledge for all teachers. In particular, teachers should be cognizant of the impact environmental factors—for example, seating arrangements—have on the development of certain kinds of friendships (Hallinan & Williams, 1987; Rizzo, 1989). The intentional rearrangement of classroom seating patterns may be one strategy a teacher can employ to encourage and foster interactions between children from different ethnic groups.

KINDERGARTEN

My recollections of kindergarten, which I attended in the 1960s, include a lengthy playtime with blocks; chocolate milk; and two lavatories—a blue door for boys and a pink door for girls. During this study, I was amazed at how kindergarten had changed from those days. I suspect parents, too, often are surprised by the changes in the kindergarten curriculum when they visit their children's classrooms.

The most recent and perhaps noticeable change is that kindergarten children today are likely to attend class for a full day. Olsen and Zigler (1989) reported that about 50% of American children attend extended kindergarten programs. This number, however, is not reflected in the schools that participated in this project—only one school had a full-day kindergarten program. The remainder of the children attended half-day sessions for approximately 2 ¾ hours per day. The latter arrangement is thought to reflect the young child's need to spend time with his or her parents and accommodate the overenrollment in some schools (e.g., Caldwell, 1989).

The School Day

A typical school day was divided into specific time frames designated for particular activities. Some of these were permanently scheduled—for example, gym and library; others could be manipulated by the teachers. The following schedule is an example of a kindergarten day:

8:45 A.M.	Morning bell
8:45-9:05 A.M.	Pledge of Allegiance
9:05-9:35 A.M.	Gym
9:35-10:05 A.M.	Worksheet/Activity
10:05-10:30 A.M.	Counting/Activity
10:30-11:00 A.M.	Playtime
11:00-11:15 A.M.	Snacktime
11:15-11:30 A.M.	Show and Tell
11:30 A.M.	Dismissal

Curriculum

In the past, the kindergarten curriculum emphasized play as the focal activity and social development as its primary task. Like the length of the school day, this focus, too, has experienced change. Kindergarten programs now emphasize academic skills, reading readiness, and preprepared worksheets (e.g., Kamii, 1985; Nall, 1982; National Association for the Education of Young Children, 1988), and the demands placed on young children participating in these programs have become a recent concern of educators, curriculum planners, and child study researchers (e.g., Elkind, 1981; Granucci, 1990; Peck, McCaig, & Sapp, 1988).

The majority of the schools visited had traditional classrooms (Barnett, 1982; Harrison, 1981; McTeer & Beaver, 1981; Silberman, 1970) in which the children were confined to their stationary seats for most of the school day. This educational philosophy is a reflection of the current "back to basics" movement in American education (Altman, 1981; Breslin, 1981; O'Bryan-Garland & Parkay, 1985). Tasks in most, if not all, cases were teacher directed and completed by the children on a large group basis. The children completed at least one worksheet each day, and each one was detached from a preprepared booklet (Smith, 1987). For example, a worksheet on shapes presented the children with a sample square, and their task was to circle all similar shapes that appeared on the page. Mickey's (Thoreau) statement reflects the children's view of these tasks: "You need a pencil, Robyn. This is work."[2]

All of the teachers expressed a desire to forego these types of tasks (e.g., Hatch & Freeman, 1988) and consistently incorporated more flexible kinds of activities into their class programs. Some of the teachers consciously devised lesson plans to circumvent large group presentations of class material. For instance, one teacher had her children work in small cooperative groups to prepare recipes for food items that began with a target alphabet letter.

Finally, the kindergarten teacher of the full-day session (Bryant) took a firm stance on creating a nontraditional classroom (Barnett, 1982; Harrison, 1981; Minuchin & Shapiro, 1983). In this class, the children often were engaged in cooperative small group projects and experiential learning tasks. The teacher's role was aimed more at guiding the child, rather than at having the child imitate the teacher's actions (Bredekamp, 1987; Moyer, Egertson, & Isenberg, 1987). Finally, music was used in all of the classrooms as either a learning tool or a soothing background accompaniment while the children were engaged in school tasks.

Now that the matters of method and setting have been discussed, the following chapters contain the children's view of racial beliefs and relationships.

NOTES

1. School population statistics may not always reflect the general population statistics for a particular township or city. This is due, in part, to a parent's option to enroll his or her child into a private or parochial school, rather than in the public school system.

2. For a sampling of the literature on the play/work dichotomy, consult Blanchard (1986), Cunningham and Wiegel (1992), and King (1982).

4

Categories and Cognition

THE PRINCIPLE OF DUALISM

Cultures all over the world organize their social cognition according to the principle of dualism (e.g., Maybury-Lewis & Almagor, 1989; Needham, 1973, 1979, 1980). The culture of childhood is no exception. Underlying the children's conception of their universe was the principle of a dualistic worldview. Social, physical, and biological realms were partitioned into pairs of complementary opposition.

The antithetical pairs listed in Table 4.1 were perceived by the children as inflexible categories, so membership in one pair of the dyad necessarily precluded inclusion in the other. By virtue of my playing with the children, Patrick (Lawrence) found cause to remark, "Hey look, Mrs. Holmes is a kid!" I wasn't simply a grown-up acting like a child; at that particular instant, I was a child. These children existed in a world where category boundaries were absolute and category members were homogeneous.

Although the presence of a general connecting motif was not essential to this ordering scheme, these dichotomous pairs served to define the children's position in their perception of the adult (macro) world and their own (micro) world. Pairs 1, 2, and 3 accomplished the latter; Pairs 4, 5, and 6 corresponded to the former.

Boy/Girl

The boy/girl antithetical pair was perhaps the most often used classificational construct. For these children, gender superseded race as the most influential factor in the self-identification process (Adair & Savage,

Table 4.1 Dualistic Constructs of the Children's Universe

1	Boy	Girl
2	Black	White
3	Are Friends	Aren't Friends
4	Big	Little
5	Grown-ups	Kids
6	Good	Bad

1973). Gender identity was the ultimate social marker, which then was reapplied to reinforce the children's developing self-conceptions (e.g., Kagan, 1984; Kohlberg, 1966). This ubiquitous principle served to organize the children's thoughts and attitudes and influenced their behavior in numerous situational contexts.

The children were quite curious about bodily functions, and evidence of contrasts between the sexes emerged from an anatomical standpoint. Kelly and Cheryl (Lawrence) offered their version of anatomy:

Cheryl Girls don't have boobs because they're not grown-up yet [simultaneously forming a woman's chest by pulling out her shirt].

Kelly [Relating the differences between girls and boys] . . . because they [boys] have something hanging down.

The comparison was extended to include appropriate dress codes, proper line formation, and play behavior. Thus once children learned the rules of inclusion for a gender category, they applied these rules to themselves (Draper, 1985; Falbo, 1980). Katy (Concord) stated the standards of fashion succinctly: "Girls wear dresses, boys wear belts." The children never intentionally crossed the ideal boundaries of fashion, and dubious articles of clothing caused an enormous amount of commotion (e.g., Kagan, 1984). During the following incident, Patrick (Lawrence) was frustrated and visibly upset.

John Hey, Patrick, you got girl sneakers on.

Patrick No I don't.

John Yes you do. If they were boys' shoes, they'd be snakeskin.

Later in the day, Roger remarked, "Hey, Patrick, those are girl sneakers." Again, Patrick emphatically denied his accusations, "No they're not.

They're for boys and girls." Not only was Patrick being attacked for the ambiguous nature of his shoes, but also he was being ridiculed by his "best friends." In essence, they were assaulting his character by questioning the gender association of his shoes (e.g., Kagan, 1984). This situation was very tense and caused Patrick much pain.

Not all situations involving gender-appropriate behavior caused the children distress. For example, Tess, Richard, Mare, and Walter (Thoreau) engaged in the following conversation while they were preparing to depart for the day.

Richard [to Tess] You wear makeup.
Tess Uh huh, and I got nail polish too.
Richard I wear makeup.
Tess You're a boy. You don't wear no makeup.
Richard [Teasing] And I wear high heels too!
Walter He's a boy. He don't wear those shoes.
Richard Uh huh, and a dress too.
Mare Only girls wear those, Richard. You ain't a girl.
Richard Yes I do. [Laughing during the entire conversation]
Tess He's a boy. He don't really do that.

In this instance, the children were exploring the boundaries of what they considered gender-appropriate behavior and were enjoying the humor of their conversation and the situation.

Segregation of the sexes was visible also in line formations. A violation of this rule always led to chastisement of the offender. Todd (Lawrence) quickly turned to inform me, "Hey, you're supposed to be in the girls' line." The girls were puzzled by my willingness to stand in the boys' line. Jenny (Concord) asked me, "Robyn, you're a girl. Why do you want to stand in the boys' line?" Thus, proper line formation served to reinforce gender identities and perhaps group solidarity.

Finally, gender was a more powerful factor than race in a child's quest either to either gain access or to be denied entrance into a group (Maccoby, 1990; Maccoby & Jacklin, 1987; Schofield, 1984). In these instances, the basis for group membership was determined exclusively by gender; a child's racial or ethnic grouping was of no consequence. For example, Gabriela (Joseph), a Latino girl, was giving out pretend invitations to her party at playtime. She distributed them to five girls: three were African

American and two were European American. When Anthony, an African American boy, asked for an invitation, Gabriela replied, "You can't come to my party. It's only for girls."

Black/White

These children were keenly aware of phenotypic qualities, such as skin color, that served as standards of comparison to differentiate themselves from others (Butler, 1989; Ramsey, 1987; Spencer, 1988). This became especially clear in the children's artwork. Julian (Concord) was drawing a self-portrait when he remarked, "I'm not black, so I'll do my face light brown." The children used the terms *black* and *white* frequently, although the terms were by no means monosemic (Keesing, 1972). Depending on the context, these terms referred either to categories of people or to the colors in a crayon box. Ricky's (an African American boy from Bryant) dialogue confirms the polysemic nature of color terms.

Inv. What do you think the word *black* means?
Ricky Uh, to be black.
Inv. What else could it mean?
Ricky It's the crayon black.

In both instances, the terms *black* and *white* for the children were complementary opposites and sometimes were used interchangeably with the antithetical pair *light/dark.*

Consider the following examples and the importance of situational contexts in which the children employed color terms. As one example, during the Parade of Colors (a listening activity in which the children responded to color cues from lyrics to a song), Kelly (Lawrence), a European American girl, mentioned to Brian, an African American boy, that he was "white." Although Kelly was referring to Brian's color sheet, Brian misinterpreted her statement. He emphatically replied, "No, I'm not. I'm black."

In this case, the misunderstanding of the use of a color term threatened Brian's developing self-conceptions, of which racial identity and awareness were important aspects (Phinney, 1989; Phinney & Rotheram, 1987; Semaj, 1985; Spencer, 1985). Thus Brian reacted accordingly and immediately clarified the matter.

As a second example, Peter (Thoreau), an African American boy, and I were discussing the meaning of the terms *white* and *black.* Peter explained, "There's real white, like Santa's beard or like chalk, but I don't like the color black. I like blue." In this instance, Peter was referring exclusively to the hue of an object. Although Peter had a dark brown complexion, he did not like the color black (see also Williams & Morland, 1976, for children's color preferences), and his choice did not distress him in any way.

Are Friends/Aren't Friends

The children were emphatic about their friend choices and persistently proclaimed and reaffirmed their friend relationships. The children were extraordinary little people because they inhabited two disparate worlds. With their peers, they were able to express their ideas and creativity. There was no fear of being silenced or reprimanded by an external source of authority. Here, children were the active participants. They alone set the standards of behavior. Play and friendship served as reinforcing guidelines on their journey to discover their identities. The children were no longer a small part of a larger, adult order; this world belonged to them.

In contrast, there was the encompassing adult world. The children found it difficult to conceive of becoming an adult. Past and future times were not realistic dimensions: As 5-year-olds, all they knew was the present (Gesell & Ilg, 1946, p. 63). Although this adult world was viewed primarily as enormous, authoritative, and intimidating, it still provided the love and security of their family. Nevertheless, the children truly believed there was only a minimal place for them here. The following antithetical pairs defined the children's position in relation to the adult (macro) world.

Big/Little

Given the children's view of adult society, it was not surprising that they described their position in terms of relative size (Corsaro, 1985). I once asked Cheryl (Lawrence) why she was always found at the end of the line. She explained that "little people" walked slower than "bigger" ones. All of the older children at school were collectively referred to as the "bigger kids." The children often compared themselves with me in regard to height. Justin (Joseph) was surprised that I was not very tall for a grown-up. He said, "Robyn, my daddy is way bigger than you. You're little like me." For children, stature, like authority, is an inherent aspect of adulthood.

Grown-Ups/Kids

"Grown-ups" always were mentioned in direct contrast to "kids" across the dimensions of size, authority, and permissible behavior. Katy (Lawrence) articulated the differences: "Children are smaller and don't say bad words. Adults are bigger, and they can say bad words without getting into trouble."

I usually sat in a small chair so that I would be level with the children when we spoke. Bryan (Concord) was amused: "You're a grown-up. You're supposed to sit in the big chair." The children often were surprised when I conversed with them about their favorite television shows. Michael (Lawrence) remarked, "You're a grown-up and you watch *Alf.* Only kids watch him." For the children, adults were expected to behave in certain ways and to enjoy privileges that children could not.

Good/Bad

These children were willing to please and took great pride in being commended for good behavior (e.g., Gesell & Ilg, 1946; Kagan, 1984). They were all too aware of the consequences for being 'bad.' At school, misbehavior incurred punishment—usually a change in seating or a verbal reprimand. Anthony (Joseph) and I were working on a coloring assignment when my attention was distracted by an event at another table that I wanted to observe. When it came time to hand in our worksheets, mine was incomplete. Anthony remarked, "Robyn, you're a bad girl. You didn't finish yours like you were supposed to." This construct was also influential in determining friendship choices. Prior classification as "bad" ultimately resulted in exclusion from play.

This introduction to how the children view their universe is necessary to understanding the principles of classification that children employ in categorizing people.

The ability to form categories is one of the most basic and fundamental cognitive processes that all human beings share (Bruner, Goodnow, & Austin, 1972). According to Bruner, Goodnow, and Austin (1956), this process serves several adaptive functions: (a) conservation of memory, (b) identification and subsequent grouping of familiar items, and (c) a technique by which we organize knowledge (see also Medin & Smith, 1984, for an overview of categorization).

Young children develop the ability to place objects and events into categories at an early age. Recent studies (Holmes, 1991a, 1992b; Mandler, 1990) have challenged the validity of Piagetian thought that claims young children are not capable of hierarchical classification. The children who participated in this study were asked, "What kinds of people do you think there are?" *People* is defined here as a natural category (Rosch, 1973; Rosch & Lloyd, 1978), and examples of such a category are colors (e.g., Berlin & Kay, 1991); cups, glasses, and mugs (e.g., Anderson, 1975; Kempton, 1978); and musical instruments (e.g., Rosch, Mervis, Gray, Johnson, & Boyes-Braem, 1976). These kinds of categories share the following properties: (a) They are found in or are characteristic of the real world; (b) they are not composed of equivalent members, so members vary by degree of representativeness with respect to a central or core member; and (c) they are hierarchical, that is, smaller categories may be subsumed into larger ones. All of the children were able to supply smaller categories that were subsumed under the larger category term *people* and to identify the attributes that distinguished one category from another.

THE CHILDREN'S CLASSIFICATION SCHEME FOR PEOPLE

By virtue of their cognitive abilities and life experiences, young children and adults do not share similar cultural knowledge about categories. Thus it is likely that in constructing a category, young children will deem certain attributes important that adults might ignore or exclude (Mervis, 1987).

A case in point is how young children structure their categories for people. As Tajfel (1981) contends, people learn about their social universe by classifying individuals and events into categories. A presumption of this classification process is that although many kinds of people exist, they can all be placed into a limited number of categories. In particular, an antithetical pair emerges: one's ingroup and the outgroup (Brome, 1989; Jones, 1983; Wilder, 1986). This distinction allows one to compare and contrast one's ingroup members with members from another group.

For children, the process of social comparison emerges in the early school years, at which time they begin to describe themselves in reference to other individuals (Butler, 1989; Ruble, 1987). They focus on salient characteristics, such as skin color, for the purpose of social comparison (Asher & Allen, 1969; Burns, 1979; Harter, 1983; Ramsey, 1987; Spencer, 1985) and to systematically classify people into groups (Aboud, 1988; Tajfel, 1981; Wilder, 1986; Williams & Morland, 1976). This was true for the children who participated in this project. They placed people into different categories primarily on the basis of skin color and the native language an individual spoke. In short, they classified people according to how they looked and how they behaved (Bullock & Lutkenhaus, 1990).

These children relied on the color terms *white, brown,* and *black* and ethnic terms, such as *Japanese* and *Spanish,* to categorize and distinguish groups of people; these terms were applied casually in their everyday speech. Because the children exist in a world that is absolute, membership in a category was unconditional, and members were believed to be homogenous. Hence a person either belonged or did not belong to a particular category. The following categories were received in response to the query, "What kinds of people do you think there are?" For example, when I asked Jenna (Concord) this question, she replied, "Some peoples are black. Some peoples are white. And some peoples are Spanish." The children's categories are listed in Table 4.2; the frequency with which they were reported appear in Table 4.3. Each category is discussed individually.

Before proceeding with the children's smaller cognitive categories of people, it seems noteworthy to mention the similarities that all members of the larger category *people* share. These children believed that all human beings, regardless of racial or ethnic membership, shared anatomical features, such as eyes, other body parts, and hair color. Some children extended the similarities to include how people should treat one another. Timmy (Concord), a European American boy, explained, "Everybody's the same, and we're supposed to be nice to all the people. It doesn't matter if they're brown or from another country."

White People

Members of the category *white people* shared one common attribute: white skin. Nevertheless, varying degrees of a person's complexion allowed them to be classified as a *white person.* The following conversation occurred during a drawing session with Tess (Thoreau), an African American girl.

Table 4.2 The Children's Categories of People

Category	*Attribute*
White[a]	White skin, "English like me"
Brown[a]	Brown skin
Black	Brown or black skin; have "real real dark skin"
Spanish	Speak Spanish, have white skin
Japanese	"Talk funny"; "Have eyes that go like this"
Chinese	Have "eyes that squint"
Other categories[b]	

a. Some of the children used the terms *light skinned* and *dark skinned* for white and brown people, respectively.
b. The categories *Jewish, Catholic, rich,* and *poor* were received as responses from only two children. One child proffered the term *mixed people* to refer to individuals who were "black and white"; one

Inv. Please tell me about white people.

Tess White people, uh, they're like white. Some people are light white, and they have bumps on their freckles. And there are dark white people. You're [the investigator] like dark white too.

Thus it seemed reasonable to suppose that the children structured this category around a prototypical member and that members were included on the basis of how far they strayed from the color of the core member (Rosch, 1973; Rosch & Lloyd, 1978). Members of this category were not "real white" and could not possess brown skin. Instead, members of this category could have whitish, pinkish, or peach complexions.

In addition, white people shared the following attributes: curly hair, any hair color, and brown or blue eyes. A white person could never have brown skin.

Brown People

The children believed that all members of the category *brown people* also shared one common attribute: brown skin. As was the case for members of the category *white people,* the color of a member's skin varied by degree with respect to a core member. Rachel (Bryant), an African American girl, explained, "We're all brown people in my family. My

Table 4.3 Percentage of Responses by School and Racial Group for Categories of People

School	Categories					
	White	*Brown*	*Black*	*Spanish*	*Chinese*	*Japanese*
Bryant						
Afr Am	94	92	10	9	4	5
Eur Am	100	100	3	4	2	2
Concord						
Afr Am	90	90	5	10	0	0
Eur Am	95	97	2	6	7	8
Joseph						
Afr Am	92	95	7	12	1	3
Eur Am	97	91	2	9	0	2
Lawrence						
Afr Am	97	95	5	2	2	0
Eur Am	100	98	3	1	1	3
Thoreau						
Afr Am	95	93	9	8	1	2
Eur Am	96	94	5	5	0	2

daddy's brown, my baby brother's darker brown, and Mommy's light brown. She's lighter than me."

For some children, membership in this category was extended to include one's spouse and children. To the query, "What do people have to have to be called 'brown'?" Tami (Joseph) replied, "They have to have a brown wife, a brown son, a brown baby, and a brown daughter." According to the children, brown people were different from black or white people because they had brown skin. Finally, a brown person could not have blond hair, straight hair, or blue eyes.

Black People

Black people was perhaps the most difficult category for the children. Some children never employed this category. Taylor (Concord) explained, "There's no such thing as a black person. Only a brown person. See, Trevor's brown." Other children recognized this category as a viable one when queried for categories of people. All members of this category had to have either black or "real dark" skin.

Some of the African American children who used this category were aware of the denotation of *black* as an identifying social marker, while other African American and European American children were not aware of the social significance of the term. The latter group's responses coincided with developmental research suggesting that young children first become aware of their skin color before they begin to comprehend that it ultimately will place them into a particular racial or ethnic group (Spencer, 1985, 1988).

For example, to the query, "Tell me, please, what makes a person a black person," Jackie (Bryant) replied, "It means to be black." This was followed by the query, "What do you mean by 'to be *black*'?" Jackie replied, "It feels good to be black." Members of this category, then, possessed more than just black or brown skin. For some of the African American children, the color black was associated with their racial identity (Semaj, 1985; Spencer, 1985, 1988).

Some children did not comprehend the social nature of the color term. To the query, "What do you think it means when somebody says 'you're black'?" Maureen (Joseph), an African American girl, replied, "People could call me black, but I'm not. I'm really brown." Some African American children were offended if a classmate referred to them as "black." Tess (Thoreau) explained, "Every day I play with black people, but my mommy said I'm pretty 'cause I'm light brown." One might suspect these types of responses were due, in part, to the children's desire to depict and describe themselves accurately to other individuals. Although the evidence is thinner than I would like, the children may have been adamant about being called brown rather than black because of the relationship between skin color preference and social desirability (Clark et al., 1980) and prejudices within the African American community involving preferential treatment for those who possess lighter skin (e.g., Russell & Wilson, 1992).

Chinese People

The children classified people as Chinese on the basis of one observable trait: the characteristic eye fold common in Asian populations. Sean (Thoreau) explained why his mom "looks a little bit like Chinese . . . 'cause her eyes look like that." As he spoke, he moved his fingers to his eyes to create a slant at the bottom of both eyebrows. In addition, Chinese people had to possess either white or yellowish skin. They could never possess brown skin.

Japanese People

The children did not use the terms *Chinese* and *Japanese* interchangeably, although members of both categories shared the common feature of the characteristic epicanthic eye fold. Ricky's (Bryant) father was in the army and stationed in Japan. To the query, "Tell me about Japanese people," Ricky replied, "My daddy's in Japan, and that's what they look like [he pulls the skin from the corner of his eye with his index finger]." In addition, the children believed that a member of this category must speak Japanese. One child had a Japanese nanny and was quite knowledgeable about Asian culture. He was an exception.

Spanish People

For these children, Spanish people had one defining characteristic: "They have to talk Spanish." They were distinguished from other categories of people because "they teach them English." Nevertheless, Spanish people shared an attribute that defined the category *white people*: Spanish people possessed white skin. A Spanish person could be white, kind of white, and darker white, but never brown or black. I found this exclusionary principle unusual, given the children's preoccupation with accurately representing themselves in self-portraits and the fact that some of the Latino children had a dark olive complexion that bordered on the hue of brown.

It seems reasonable to suppose that young children are quite capable of classifying people into smaller order categories (Holmes, 1991a, 1992b; Mandler, 1990). The principles by which they do so are based fundamentally on observable characteristics such as skin color or the language one speaks (Aboud, 1988; Burns, 1979; Harter, 1983; Ramsey, 1987). In this instance, it seems likely that young children in the process of categorizing people into groups may emphasize attributes such as skin color that an adult might overlook or ignore entirely (Mervis, 1987). Thus adults working with young children should be cognizant of the fact that children, because of their cognitive abilities, may be focusing on different attributes when conversing and interacting with peers from differing racial and ethnic groups.

What is striking is the children's prevalent use of color terms to categorize people and the polysemic nature that some of these terms possess (e.g.,

Keesing, 1972). The concern with developing a multicultural curriculum, coupled with children's preoccupation with accurately depicting themselves in artistic creations, has inspired some manufacturers to develop learning tools, such as the new Crayola assortment of crayons that contains the skin nuances for various cultural groups. Such tools foster discussions concerning the similarities and differences that human beings share.

Finally, the children's cognitive structuring for categories of people appears to follow the principles associated with natural categories—namely, that children structure their categories around the notion of a core member (e.g., Rosch, 1973; Rosch et al., 1976). Thus membership in the categories varies by degree along the continuum of color in those instances in which the children employ skin color as the identifying attribute of the category. Discussions that center on learning about racial and cultural groups may serve to broaden children's existing knowledge of categories of people by emphasizing attributes other than superficial or overt characteristics (see Wieseman, 1986, for a discussion of issues associated with multiculturalism in educational contexts and environments).

5

Conceptions of Self

Children do not enter the world with a conception of self. Rather, this cognitive notion develops as children mature (Bandura, 1986). First, infants need to become aware that they are unique, independent, and separate from other individuals and can have an influence on their surroundings (Bandura, 1986; Bertenthal & Fisher, 1978). By age 2, children can recognize themselves in a mirror (Amsterdam, 1972; Harter, 1988; Lewis & Brooks-Gunn, 1979). By age 2 ½, the process is complete, and children now see themselves as separate and autonomous from other individuals (Neisser, 1988).

The process does not end here, however, for the development of the self-concept is complex. It includes the acquisition of gender and racial identities (Phinney, 1989; Semaj, 1985; Spencer, 1988) and an awareness of one's own personal characteristics (McCandless & Evans, 1973).

As Piaget (1965) contended, the content of the self-concept and the way children process and convey information about themselves is linked with cognitive maturation (Branch & Newcombe, 1986; Semaj, 1985; Spencer, 1985). In early childhood, children describe themselves in terms of membership in certain groups defined by physical characteristics, "I have brown skin" (Burns, 1979; Harter, 1983); possessions, "I have an umbrella" (Damon & Hart, 1982); and gender, "I am a boy" (Damon & Hart, 1988). Emphasis thus is placed on typical qualities, rather than on those employed in social comparisons; this emphasis stems from emerging cognitive abilities in which children become aware of their skin color before they come to learn that one's skin color ultimately will determine their racial or ethnic membership (Semaj, 1985; Spencer, 1988). For example, a young child's statement that he or she has "brown skin" is not linked with the fact that the child will be socially labeled in our society as African American (Spencer, 1988). It is during the early and middle school years that children begin describing themselves in reference to others (Butler, 1989; Ruble, 1987).

In addition, young children's conceptions of self may contain personal preferences and particular physical attributes (Harter, 1988). Although older children, because of increasing cognitive and social skills, describe themselves in terms of personality traits and characteristics (Kagan, 1984), one should not conclude that young children are not capable of including psychological criteria in their self-conceptions (Eder, 1989; Eder, Gerlack, & Perlmutter, 1987). Recent research (Eder, 1990; Estes, Wellman, & Wooley, 1989; Johnson & Wellman, 1982) suggests that young children possess knowledge of themselves that extends beyond superficial characteristics such as physical appearance and personal activities.

The discussion of the children's conceptions of self contained in this chapter is based exclusively on the data collected from conversations while the children were drawing their self-portraits (e.g., Coles, 1964).

SELF-PORTRAITS AND CONCEPTIONS OF SELF

The children described themselves according to findings reported in the existing literature on children's conceptions of self. They often concentrated on physical characteristics, gender, and personal possessions in compiling their self-conceptions. Also, the children did not differentiate themselves from their physical surroundings. Thus self-descriptions contained information about where the children lived, specific possessions or articles of clothing, and gossip about family members (Bullock & Lutkenhaus, 1990).

I asked Michele (Joseph), a European American girl (see Figure 5.1), to tell me about herself while she was drawing. She replied, "I have brown eyes. I'm a girl. I have hair, and my teeth are white, and my tongue is red, and my cheeks are a little red. I like to play with dolls."

Maria (Thoreau), a Latino girl (see Figure 5.2), explained what was important in telling someone about herself. She began, "I have clothes. I have some long hair, ah, and I play with my brother . . . I play with my baby cousin. Her name is Katie, and I go over to my aunt's house. I sleep at my aunt's house, and then I watch a movie."

Figure 5.1. A self-portrait by Michele.

One major difference between European American and African American children emerged while they were creating and describing their self-portraits: All of the African American children emphasized clearly the color of their skin when describing their pictures. By contrast, only two of the European American children did. Most of the European American children focused on other details and attributes in describing themselves.

Consider, for example, Julie's (an African American girl from Bryant) description of her self-portrait (see Figure 5.3). She began, "My face is all brown, and my hair is all black, and I have a hat on, and there goes my neck [she points to the picture]—my brown neck, and I have a black body, and I have a brown foot."

Doug (Concord), an African American boy, offered to draw his picture for me without hesitation (see Figure 5.4).

Inv. Please tell me about Doug. If I were someone you didn't know, what would be important to tell me all about you?

Doug I have a brown face and black eyes, a round stomach, and new shoes, and new pants, and a new shirt, too.

Inv. Is it important to tell someone you have a brown face?

Doug My mom tells me I gotta tell everybody about my brown face.

Figure 5.2. A self-portrait by Maria.

Inv. Why do you think she tells you that?

Doug I don't know.

Inv. What are Mommy and Daddy like?

Doug Daddy's peach [a color term the children employed to describe complexions ranging from olive to light brown], and he has black hair. I'm brown, and I have black hair.

In these instances, the African American children made a clear point of emphasizing physical attributes, in particular, nuances of skin color,

Figure 5.3. A self-portrait by Julie.

before proceeding with the other details of their self-descriptions. One might conclude tentatively that, for these children, skin color is not simply an overt and recognizable characteristic. Rather, it is one that helps them develop a sense of self and personal and group identity (e.g., Cross, 1985; Semaj, 1985; Spencer, 1982, 1984, 1985). This notion may explain why all of these children found it necessary to provide the investigator with this information.

In addition, the children's desire to emphasize their skin color in their self-portrait descriptions may be a consequence of sociocultural influences (e.g., Damon & Hart, 1988; Levine & White, 1986). In American

Figure 5.4. A self-portrait by Doug.

culture, racial and ethnic categories are immutable, and membership is determined by skin color or ethnic heritage. Young children come to acquire this cultural knowledge at an early age. Thus for African American children, who are children of color, emphasizing the attribute of skin color in their descriptions of their self-portraits may be more important in expressing their conceptions of self than conveying details about their personal experiences (Cross, 1985; Harter, 1983; Spencer, 1988).

Only one African American girl did not make any reference to her skin color in describing herself, and she was the only child of color not to do so. When asked to tell the investigator about herself, Meredith (Joseph) responded with, "I have a face, hands, fingers, and clothes."

Finally, it is particularly worthy of mention how these African American children viewed their own self-image and evaluated their self-esteem. In contrast to interpretations from research conducted prior to the mid-1960s that concluded that young African American children possessed low self-esteem (Clark, 1966; Morland, 1966; Slaughter & McWorter, 1985; Spencer, 1988), the children of this study had a strong and proud sense of their personal and group identity (Branch & Newcombe, 1986; Cross, 1985; Semaj, 1985; Spencer, 1985). The following conversation with Terri (Bryant) supports this contention.

Inv. How do you feel about white people?
Terri Good.
Inv. How do you feel about brown or black people?
Terri I'm brown, and I feel good about me and other people like me.

While Mickey (Thoreau) and I were drawing together, I asked him, "What does it mean to you to be black?" He replied, "It feels real good to be black." I continued, "Why does it feel real good?" Mickey continued, "'Cause black people are good, and you get more friends. I gots lots of friends." Recent research findings (Bowman & Howard, 1985; Branch & Newcombe, 1986; Spencer, 1983) suggest that parents play a crucial role in shaping their children's racial attitudes and that active intervention strategies by African American parents may be a contributing factor to raising children with strong conceptions of self and self-esteem.

My brief interactions at school with the parents of these African American children support this contention. For example, conversations with these parents at extracurricular school activities, Parents' Day, and Open House revealed that approximately half of these adults were actively teaching their children about their African heritage and African American culture.

All of the children knew who Dr. Martin Luther King Jr. was because he was discussed in all of the schools, but the parents from Bryant and

Thoreau Schools also discussed the civil rights leader at home. Some of the parents from Bryant, Thoreau, and Concord Schools also taught their children about African cultural traditions, such as Kwanzaa (a festive celebration occurring in late December) and arts and crafts. Shawny (Bryant), an African American girl, wore a traditional necklace from Ghana that her mother helped Shawny make at home.

Although all the children taught me much about how they view the world, I learned one of the most genuine lessons from Stefan (Bryant) in the following conversation. I asked him, "How does it feel to be black?" Stefan replied, "I don't know, Robyn. It feels like a person. I'm just a person, and that's all I know." I wondered how I as an adult would have answered the same question. I came to the same conclusion as Stefan. I'm not really certain what it feels like to be the color white and have never given this fact any thought. It seems reasonable to suppose that, for children and adults, being a color is equated with just being a person.

A 5-year-old's candid response provided a possible solution for achieving racial harmony: Every individual is a person, not a black, brown, or white one, and every individual should be treated similarly because we are all human beings. I was abashed that my query seemed to highlight the distinctions among people (Wilder, 1986), yet was cognizant of the fact that as children mature and are influenced by external conditions—for example, parental behavior (e.g., Branch & Newcombe, 1986; Raman, 1984) and peers—they begin to learn and internalize notions of group stereotypes and prejudices (Devine, 1989; Miller, 1982; Quattrone, 1986).

Of all the African American children interviewed, only one child, a girl, expressed a desire not to be a member of her ethnic group. Trish (Joseph) and I had the following conversation about white and brown people.

Trish I wish I was white. I wish I was like you.
Inv. Why do you wish you were like me?
Trish 'Cause I wanna be light, but I like white people and brown people.

The motivating factor in this case, I think, was the child's desire to have a lighter brown skin, rather than to be white. This conclusion is based partly on Trish's positive responses to questions regarding how she felt about members of her own racial ingroup, the fact that her classmates commented on her very dark complexion, and the fact that the children categorized me as having "peach" or "not real white skin." The issue of prejudices within the African American community with regard to one's complexion was addressed briefly in Chapter 4 (e.g., Russell & Wilson, 1992).

By contrast, consider how Dicky (Concord), a European American boy, described himself while he was drawing for me (see Figure 5.5).

> **Inv.** If you were to describe yourself, how would you do that? Please tell me about Dicky.
>
> **Dicky** Um, I have a sister, and her name is Jamie, like Jamie in our class. And I have a boat—my dad's boat, not mine. My sister has a boat, a little boat.

Greg (Lawrence), a European American boy (see Figure 5.6), also focused on personal information, rather than on skin color. The following are excerpts from a conversation that lasted an entire play period.

> **Inv.** Please draw a picture of yourself, and while you're drawing, could you please tell me about yourself.
>
> **Greg** This is the tree at my house. I have this tree and I wanted to climb it a little. I have a friend who comes over to my house and climbs it with me.
>
> **Inv.** Those are your feet [he points for the investigator to name them]. . . . Did you use blue because you have blue eyes?
>
> **Greg** Yeah, my whole family does. . . . My dad's a builder.
>
> **Inv.** Greg, you didn't color your face in. You left it white. Is that important that you leave it white? [He proceeds to color his face in brown.] Why did you color it brown?
>
> **Greg** 'Cause, I, how could I make myself white? If I was white, there'd be nothing there [the paper he is drawing on is white], so that's why I colored it like that. 'Cause if I didn't, if I was white, that wouldn't be good because this piece of paper would be plain and there would only be trees. So that's the real test. Yesterday, I played with my soccer friends, and we went to this party.

The children often took great pains in representing themselves accurately in their artwork. They carefully chose crayons that they felt would make their drawings as realistic as possible. Mickey (Thoreau) and I were coloring in a page of our art books for a class project when he offered to color part of mine for me. He said, "I'll do your hair brown 'cause that's the color it really is." When Bob (Bryant) was coloring in a person from his worksheet, he remarked to his tablemate Jack, "I'm not going to color mine [the face]. I'm leaving mine white 'cause I'm white." Jack replied,

Figure 5.5. A self-portrait by Dicky.

"You're not white. I'm not white. Look [pointing to his arm], you're pinkish tan."

In these instances, children of color often searched for the closest shade of brown or black for skin color, whereas European American children

Figure 5.6. A self-portrait by Greg.

usually opted for white or yellow when depicting themselves in self-portraits. Christian (Concord), an African American boy, asked me to draw a picture of him that he could keep. The following conversation we had while I was drawing his portrait illustrates the children's desires to draw themselves or to have others draw them in accurate detail.

Christian Look at me, and then you could draw me.

Because he had colored me purple, I asked him whether I could use the same color to draw him. The query prompted this exchange.

Christian I'm brown, so do me brown. Everybody's talking about I'm black, but I'm really brown. It's okay. You can color me any color you want, but I'm brown for real.

Inv. What should I do about your hair?

Christian It's black, but don't draw it sticking up 'cause it doesn't look like that. Draw it right, okay? And don't give me red lips 'cause I don't wear lipstick.

Inv. I promise I won't.

Christian And I got an earring, so don't forget to put that in too. [I drew a star in his left earlobe on the portrait to represent the diamond earring Christian actually wore in his left earlobe.]

When the children were asked to draw peers from racial or ethnic outgroups, all employed similar strategies when attempting to depict them. Variations from accurate representations were due, in part, to lack of the correct materials and the children's creative desires to use colors that were unexpected. I once asked Kim (Concord), a European American girl, why she was using yellow to outline her face. "I'm really peach, but we don't have that color here, so I'm using yellow."

THE CHILDREN'S CONCEPTIONS OF OTHERS

Because the first part of this chapter was devoted to the children's conceptions of self, it seems appropriate to discuss also the children's conceptions of individuals who possessed membership in ethnic groups to which the children did not belong (e.g., Brome, 1989). The following material contains African American children's knowledge of European Americans and European American children's knowledge of African Americans.

African American Children's Views of European Americans

Most of the African American children in this sample expressed ambivalent feelings about European Americans when asked to make generalizations about them. This ambivalence stood in direct contrast to the children's responses about particular friends or individuals who were members of this group. It is possible that this kind of cognitive reasoning parallels the children's process of acquiring a personal and group identity. For example, the formation of the self-concept and a concept of others is linked developmentally with cognitive maturation and prior socialization experiences (Cross, 1985; Phinney, 1989; Spencer, 1988). It seems plausible, then, that these factors may affect how children acquire concepts of outgroups and their individual members. As Aboud and Skerry (1984) contended, the development of ethnic attitudes parallels development in cognitive processing, such as the differentiation between individuals and groups. This similarity provides an explanation for why the kindergarten children attribute characteristics of only a few individuals to the entire outgroup, yet are capable of describing particular individuals without making generalizations or comparisons to the group (e.g., Judd & Park, 1988; Sigelman & Welch, 1993; Spencer, 1988).

Consider the following dialogue that occurred between Jerry (Bryant) and me during playtime. It was one of the most illuminating conversations I had with the children during my research.

Jerry Sometimes black people and white people don't like each other.

Inv. Why do you think that?

Jerry A man shot Martin Luther King. We celebrated his birthday at my house.

Inv. How did you celebrate it?

Jerry Uh, 'cause my mom and what my teacher told me about Martin Luther King. They told me he was shot by a white man and he didn't like him so he shot him for no reason. And they caught him.

Inv. That's true. Martin Luther King Jr. was shot by a white man. Do you think all white people don't like black people then?

Jerry I know where he was standing when he was shot. It was sad because he was watching the black people and white people Americans. He was the most wonderful man in the world, and somebody just shot him for no reason.

Inv. Do you think all white people don't like black people because of this?

Jerry I don't know. But the one that shot him was mean.

This conversation arose, in part, because of the teacher's discussion about Martin Luther King Jr. and the child's conversation with his parents. His dialogue revealed his conceptions and knowledge of King's assassination and his subjective feelings for King and the man who assassinated him. Such personal interpretations provide clues about how children acquire racial attitudes and form conceptions about their own and other racial and ethnic groups. Jerry had a strong sense of self, in part because of his parents' teachings and positive experiences with his peers.

One of the most common adjectives used by the African American children to describe white people was *mean.* But *mean* in this instance did not refer to disposition. Rather, it referred to an outcome of a personal situation that involved the child, and this adjective was applied to both brown and white people. Consider Terri's (Bryant) example.

Terri Some white people are mean. Because some white people sometimes, because some white people don't like black people and they're mean. The other day I was walking to school. I saw this little white girl and I said "Hi" and then she said "Hi" and I thought she liked me and she did 'cause she played with me. One day, I was playing with this white girl and her mommy said I couldn't play with her no more. She was mean.

Inv. Are all white people mean?

Terri Not all, only some. You're never mean, Robyn. You always play with us.

In agreement with Spencer (1988), I found that the children's socialization experiences were primary factors affecting their subjective feelings about and conceptions of racial and ethnic outgroup members. Although it was difficult for the children to separate their feelings and attitudes when asked about racial or ethnic outgroups in general (e.g., see related work with adolescents by Biafora, Taylor, Warheit, Zimmerman, & Vega, 1993), their stable personal, interracial relationships with their classmates were always spoken of as positive, pleasant, and nice (e.g., Sigelman & Welch, 1993). White people were mean, but individual white friends or acquaintances with whom the children enjoyed positive experiences were never described in a negative fashion. Such reasoning may be a consequence of young children's inabilities to engage in deductive thinking (Piaget, 1965). Rather, these children concentrated on particular individuals and events when forming conceptions about groups of people.

Similar findings emerged from Schofield's (1984, 1986) work with preadolescents in a desegregated middle school. Interview material from her work with older children revealed that certain negative behaviors and characteristics were generalized and attributed to all members of a racial outgroup exclusively on the basis of their group membership. However, subjective positive feelings about specific interracial relationships and outgroup members emerged when the older children were asked to describe particular individuals and interracial friendships. Thus younger and older children can distinguish their positive feelings about individual outgroup members from stereotypical notions that emerge when they are asked to make generalizations about an entire group of people (e.g., Aboud & Skerry, 1984).

The interpretation of the data from my study with kindergarten children and Schofield's (1984, 1986) work with preadolescents is supported by social psychological and developmental research. First, the predilection to perceive members of one's own ingroup as variable and outgroup members as homogeneous has been well documented (Judd & Park, 1988; Quattrone, 1986; Simon & Brown, 1987). Thus an individual comes to infer that all members of an outgroup behave similarly, when in reality, the behavior may be linked with only a few members (e.g., Quattrone & Jones, 1980; Wilder, 1978).

It seems reasonable to conclude that the kindergarten children of this study (and the older children studied by Schofield) were acting according to this cognitive principle in perceiving category members as homogeneous. For example, the kindergarten children attributed certain behaviors or attitudes to all white people, such as "white people are mean," even though this assessment may have been based on their experiences with only a few members of this group. By contrast, this group generalization could be altered if the children had prior positive experiences with individual outgroup members. This would support my contention that the children's socialization experiences play a crucial role in the formation of attitudes about individual outgroup members.

Second, the children in both studies were able to transcend and overcome outgroup biases by describing individuals or individual interracial relationships (e.g., Hewitt, 1986; Sigelman & Welch, 1993). For example, white people were "mean," but interracial relationships that the children had formed were described in positive terms. Perhaps the treatment of an outgroup member as an individual has been effective in reducing outgroup biases because it serves to emphasize the commonalities ingroup and outgroup members share (Wilder, 1978, 1986; Worchel, Axsom, Ferris,

Samaha, & Schweitzer, 1978). It seems plausible that the children came to view outgroup members as individuals because of positive experiences during the development of their personal interracial relationships.

I asked the children, "Do you treat white children different than brown children?" Although approximately 80% said they treated all children the same, some African American children (primarily from Joseph and Concord Schools) said they treated European American children differently. Maureen (Joseph) replied, "Yeah, because white people are a different color than I am and because some black people, real black people, are black but I'm not the same color. I'm brown." Of course, the real issue here is not whether the children reported that they treated children differently because of their skin color, but whether they actually were observed to do so. I did not witness an event in which a child treated an outgroup member differently or precluded him or her from participating in an activity because of racial or ethnic membership.

It seems reasonable to suppose that (a) the children's notions of racial and ethnic outgroup members are based on personal interactions and that these notions are altered when the children encounter other similar individuals who treat them differently (Piaget, 1965; Schofield, 1984, 1986; Spencer, 1988; Wilder, 1986), and (b) African American children emphasize their skin color in their self-descriptions perhaps because they are learning to recognize and reinforce the attributes perpetuated by American society in classifying its members (Damon & Hart, 1988; Levine & White, 1986).

European American Children's Views of African Americans

The European American children with whom I worked had relatively little knowledge and apparently little contact with African Americans outside the context of school. When I asked the children how they felt about "brown people," it was not uncommon for me to receive a response such as, "I don't know much about brown people. The only brown person I know is _____ [a child in class]." Meg (Lawrence) responded, "I don't know anything about brown people. I only know they must have brown babies." Thus European American children had less social experience with African Americans and thus could supply little information.

When asked, "Do you treat white children and brown children differently?" most of the children replied they did not. A typical response to this query was, "No, they're the same." Leigh (Concord) expanded on this answer: "Brown and white, they're both the same. My daddy's got brown skin. He plays with me like my friends, so I treat them the same."

Most of the children responded in an unprejudiced fashion. Three children in particular, however, expressed prejudiced notions with regard to children of color. I asked Casey (Joseph) if he treated brown and white children differently; he replied, "Yeah, the black boy could be hiding weapons for his army, so he's bad. The white boy is good." His statement supported my observations of interactions with his peers. Casey did not interact frequently with his African American classmates either during free play or at other voluntary opportune times. Thus it seems reasonable to conclude that he was indeed prejudiced. The inclination to misperceive and transform an outgroup member into the enemy or "bad guy" was documented in the classic study on intergroup conflict called "Robbers Cave" by Sherif, Harvey, White, Hood, and Sherif (1961). It seems possible that young children also may call on this cognitive principle when interacting with outgroup members.

Diane (Concord) answered the same query, "Yeah, 'cause they're different. One's brown and one's white. They're not the same." However, Diane was observed to interact quite comfortably with racial ingroup and outgroup members in class. Thus I am hesitant to suggest that she was prejudiced as Casey was. Rather, I think her statement is calling attention to the fact that she notes a difference between brown and white children.

Finally, Sydney (Thoreau) gave the following response to the same query: "Yeah, 'cause my mommy and daddy said to." Although reared presumably in a prejudiced household, Sydney was not observed to treat racial ingroup and outgroup members differently. Thus for this child, as with Diane, there was a discrepancy between her verbal response and her observed behavior (Agar, 1980).

It seems reasonable to suppose that these children's prejudiced attitudes and behaviors are due to a number of factors that include the following:

- prejudices against certain primary colors (Spencer, 1988; Williams & Morland, 1976)
- the children's preoccupation with comparing themselves with others on the basis of observable differences (Butler, 1989; Harter, 1983; Ramsey, 1987)
- the children's extraction of information from adult conversations (Aboud, 1988)
- the fact that children are more likely to learn prejudice through observation of parental and other individuals' behavior (Bandura, 1977; Bryne, 1965; Raman, 1984; Van Evra, 1990)

the fact that residential segregation is still prevalent because these children had limited contact and social experiences with African Americans and thus had little, if any, knowledge of this group

the emergence of cognitive processes related to intergroup behavior, such as stereotypical notions, individuation of outgroup members, and the perception of outgroup members as homogeneous (Miller, 1982; Quattrone, 1986; Wilder, 1986)

media influences

The last factor requires expansion.

Racial Attitudes and the Media

In 1986, Hearold reported that the average 18-year-old spent more time viewing television than he or she did in class. Many researchers have examined the powerful effects that television viewing has had on human cognition and behavior and on its function as a socializing agent (Carey, 1989; Comstock & Paik, 1991; Lodziak, 1986; Van Evra, 1990).

The social influence of television on children's cognition and behavior is a matter of particular importance because children and teenagers cite television as an important source of information and attitudes about their own and other ethnic and racial groups (Anderson & Collins, 1988; Comstock & Paik, 1991). Nevertheless, although television is viewed often by young children, researchers in cognitive development have not yet considered television viewing to be a prominent factor in a child's social experiences (Anderson & Collins, 1988).

The results of research on the influence of television on child development are still ambiguous. This lack of clarity stems primarily from the fact that it is difficult to determine what young children are attending to when they watch television and what precisely they are learning (Anderson & Collins, 1988). It seems plausible that young children, because of their developing cognitive abilities, are unable to integrate and comprehend much of what they view (Anderson & Smith, 1984). Rather, they are attracted to the salient features of television programming, such as animation, music, and sound effects (Calvert & Gersh, 1987). How, then, does young children's viewing television affect their racial beliefs?

It seems logical to suppose that a child's developmental level strongly determines how he or she interprets the content of a program; this is one avenue through which television can affect children's racial attitudes (Van Evra, 1990). In 1986, Greenberg reported that half of the television programs did not include any minorities and that races were divided more often than they were portrayed together. Greenberg (1986) emphasized that the way minorities are portrayed is important in affecting children's attitudes. Thus children viewing minorities as participating only in crimes or low-paying occupations are likely to conclude and generalize that this must be true for all members of the group; thus prejudices and stereotypical beliefs are perpetuated (Devine, 1989).

The effects of television viewing on children's racial beliefs and attitudes occurs for both ingroup and outgroup members in relation to the children's group membership; such viewing also may have positive outcomes on racial attitudes (e.g., Johnston, 1982). European American children accept African American characters and name them as people they would like to be (Comstock & Paik, 1991). These findings support the mass appeal of athletes such as Michael Jordan to young children from various racial and ethnic groups. Such individuals are able to cross and break down racial barriers, in part, because they appeal to and highlight the commonalities that children of all colors share (Wilder, 1986). Regardless of the negative and positive effects television viewing may have on children's racial attitudes and perceptions, however, scarce attention has been given to this topic and more research is needed in this area, as Stroman (1986) suggested.

Finally, it seems noteworthy that most of the young children in this study possess positive self-esteem, are proud of their personal and group identities, and are quite able to articulate their self-conceptions. Adults should be cognizant of the fact that children not only are developing a sense of self but also are forming conceptions of others. It is vitally important that those responsible for the emotional, social, and cognitive development of our children provide them with knowledge that will enable them to become productive and compassionate members of our society who appreciate and value the differences and similarities among human beings.

6

Friendship and Ethnicity

COGNITIVE NOTIONS OF FRIENDSHIP

Friendship and *friendly* were incomprehensible terms for most of the children, presumably because of the abstract nature of these concepts. Todd (Lawrence), a European American boy, was able to explain the difference between the terms *friend* and *friendship.* He said, "There's friends. A friend is someone you like to play with, and then there's friendship. That's when people you like to do things with and you like to be with them. Sometimes you can play with them when they're there, and sometimes you can't, but that's okay." Fortunately, the children had no difficulty when it came time to discussing their friends.

One of the most pervasive aspects of children's peer cultures is the energy expended by its members to establish and maintain friend relations (e.g., Corsaro, 1985; Corsaro & Eder, 1990; Fine, 1987; Rizzo, 1989). For the children in this project, friends were viewed as treasured possessions likened to wealth, as Martina's (Lawrence) remark suggests: "I'm rich. I have plenty of friends." The reasons were apparent. Play was a beloved activity often requiring companions, so friends became a prized commodity. Murray (Thoreau) explained why he had friends: "To play ball with, have fun with, and ride bicycles."

According to Gesell and Ilg (1946, p. 66), 5-year-olds usually define articles in terms of use. I found this was also true for the definition of people. For example, Kevin (Lawrence) defined the word *friend:* "You play with them, you go over to his house, you could sleep over. That's what friends are for."

Although Kevin's summation was a bit elaborate, all of the children shared the monosemic conception of friend as "someone you play with" (e.g., Corsaro, 1985; Rubin, 1980; Selman, 1990). No wonder the children used the adjective *sad* to describe a world without friends. Although some children were content to play in solitude, most of the children preferred to play with companions. Because friends were, by definition, playmates, these children were a vital resource. Sharon (Lawrence) needed a player to complete her playgroup. She immediately ran to her friend Cheryl: "We need you to play." In essence, friends were a necessity. Otherwise, a child was forced to play alone. This possibility helped explain why the children needed constantly to proclaim friendship ties and why friendships were guarded so jealously (e.g., Corsaro, 1985; Deegan, 1991).

To the children, any individual who played with them could potentially be called a "friend," given their definition of the term. Hence they made no verbal distinctions between playmates and the children they selected as friends. In accordance with their definition of friend, the labeling process became circular, in a sense, such that by virtue of playing together, all of the children were called "friends" (e.g., Jacobsen, 1975).

Nevertheless, the children's behavior clearly indicated a preferential distinction between playmates sporadically joined for a specific purpose, on the one hand, and those children voluntarily selected as friends, on the other. Although all of these children received the same label—"friend"—and were considered members of this category, they were not treated equivalently. The latter case implied specific obligations and behavioral expectations. This represented the *core meaning* of the category, to borrow Rosch's (1973) term, which served to confirm her notion of focality in which categorical members vary by degree of representativeness with respect to the "clearest cases" or focal members.

ORGANIZING PRINCIPLES

Several organizing principles pervaded the children's notions of friendship. One principle pertained to availability, measured in terms of play interactions, and the children adjusted their behavior toward friends accordingly. Those children in class not named as friends were greeted in a cordial manner, and their behavior approximated that of neighbors (Kurth, 1970). Children voluntarily selected as friends received preferential treatment. They sought each other's company, formed conspicuous pairs or groups at playtime, and most important, complied with the rules of the friend relationship (e.g., Deegan, 1991, 1993).

Traveling further along this continuum of availability were "best friends," who shared recurrent play rights. At school, best friends were inseparable. Compliance with the rules of friendship, such as playing together and a genuine concern for one another, was paramount, and the refusal to share was considered an intolerable offense (e.g., Argyle & Henderson, 1984; Deegan, 1991). Similarly, "best friends from home" were always described as residing in close proximity (Hays, 1985). In this context, the children enjoyed recurrent play rights in their neighborhoods. In some instances, the children reported that a specific child was a friend at home and school.

A second principle was that of similarity. The children's conception of a friend was a child who was similar to them. Children are no different from adults in that they often are attracted to others with whom they share similarities (e.g., Drewry & Clark, 1984; Magaro & Ashbrook, 1985). Thus friends were compared and classified as being the same or different, in contrast with the children's self-conceptions. Sharon (Lawrence) found cause to remark on Chas's (an African American boy) arrival to class: "Now Oliver [also African American] can have a best friend his same color." At this point, Oliver already had established best friend relations in class with European American children, so race was not an issue. Instead, Sharon's astute observations suggested that the children's focal image of a best friend was one similar to how they perceive themselves. In short, children often perceive, select, and identify with friends who are similar to themselves (e.g., Arkin & Burger, 1980; Caspi & Herbener, 1990; Feingold, 1988; Magaro & Ashbrook, 1985).

This notion of a focal image also operated across the gender line. Examination of Kevin's earlier quote revealed the operative word *his*. Similarly, Todd employed the pronoun *his* in describing how to make friends. This finding supports the hypothesis that the term *friend* is synonymous with a same-sex companion.

However, this cognitive notion crossed the boundaries of race and gender. Race, ethnicity, and gender were not salient determinants of friendship choices. Rather, these existed along with the dimensions of age, locale, and physical attributes as a means of linguistically distinguishing friends. Friends were described by superficial characteristics, such as skin color, clothing color, or anatomical features, particularly when the children were drawing and wished to create accurate representations. Deegan (1991, 1993) reported similar findings in his examination of older children's friendships. This principle appears to develop early and remains stable during the middle school years. The importance of attitudinal and moral similarities as a determinant of friendship selection surfaces with increasing cognitive maturity (e.g., Caspi & Herbener, 1990; Feingold, 1988; Maccoby, 1990). Thus, for young children, race and gender do not appear to affect friendship choices.

Katy (Lawrence) and I had several discussions about best friends. Her expressed feelings and recollection of details were consistent throughout the year. Our first conversation centered on best friend choices. Katy replied:

> Heidi, but she's different. She's not in my class here. She has to wear special clothes to school, but she's the same age as me. She lives right across the street from my house. You go down my driveway, around the curve, then over the street to her house. Her nickname is "Heidi Beidi." . . . Know what? Her mom's name is Mary, and her daddy's name is Alf. She has a sister, Kerri, like my brother, Willie. He's not a newborn, he's two and a half, and she also has a new baby sister named Ellen, and she's cute.

Several months later, Katy again spoke of her friend from home.

> My best friend from the outside is Heidi. She has a new baby sister like me, except I have a new baby brother, and her name is Ellen. She [Heidi] has to wear a uniform to school. She doesn't go to a school where you can wear clothes.

Descriptions such as these revealed the children's subjective feelings about particular relationships and their cognitive notions of what a best friend is. Finally, such temporal accounts also served to support the contention that young children's friendships often remain stable throughout the school year (e.g., Berndt & Hoyle, 1985).

TAXONOMY OF FRIEND TERMS

Before proceeding with the children's folk terms for kinds of friends, several classificatory matters concerning this paradigm need to be clarified. First, classification was not judgmental or evaluative. No category was seen as superior or inferior in relation to another. Rather, all categories were perceived and treated as equivalent because they fulfilled the general criterion of being a playmate.

Second, membership in some friend categories was not absolute. Instead, membership varied by degree of representativeness (Rosch, 1973; Rosch & Lloyd, 1978). Thus, although taxonomic ranking between categories was not applicable, some categories were ranked internally through gradations of membership.

Third, not all of the children subscribed to this general paradigm. Subtle variations existed regarding the inclusion of the contrasting categories *parents* and *teachers.* For some children, either parents or teachers (never both categories) were excluded from the domain *friends* because of the functions (roles) they performed. Other children took this one step farther and viewed *friends* as an exclusive domain that included only smaller categories of friends.

CATEGORIES OF FRIENDS

The friend categories that appeared most frequently in the children's casual speech appear in Table 6.1 and are discussed below.

Girlfriends/Boyfriends

Members of the category *girlfriends/boyfriends* possessed a special beauty and a certain attraction that distinguished them from same-sex dyads of classmates. Children are no different from adults insofar as physical attractiveness is a powerful determinant of a romantic partner (e.g., Baron & Byrne, 1991; Dion, 1980). More important, these children engaged in the activity of kissing and were perceived as potential marriage partners. This relationship, discussed at greater length later in this chapter, was quite embarrassing to its participants, an emotional quality never associated with other cross-sex friendships.

Best Friends

Members of the category *best friends* possessed the following attributes: (a) availability (recurrent play rights) and/or proximity; (b) intimate knowledge of each other; (c) similarity, measured through self-conceptions; and (d) likability, usually expressed in terms of niceness.

Best friends enjoyed exclusive dyadic relationships in which adherence to the rules of friendship was paramount. Children involved in this

Table 6.1 List of Folk Categories Included in the Domain *Friends*

		Girl-boyfriends (romantic)
Friends	Smaller, inclusive categories of friends	Best friends[a]
		Good friends
		Friends, buddies,[b] girlfriends[c]
		Friends from home
Family	Inclusive contrasting categories of family members and teachers	Parents
		Brothers
		Sisters
		Cousins
Teachers		Teachers (familiar and unfamiliar)
		Principal

a. This category is internally ranked.
b. This term is interchangeable with the term *friend.*
c. This term refers to a friend and distinguishes this "friend" from others on the basis of gender.

relationship were inseparable at school. They even went so far as to push an intruding classmate out of line formation so as not to come between the children who selected each other as best friends. This was one of the few categories that possessed an internal ranking system.

Good Friends

The category *good friends* was used as a stepping stone between the developmental sequence leading from friend to best friend. A good friend was usually a neighbor who lived nearby and who played with the children at home. Although not worthy of being a best friend, these children were more than just friends.

Friends

Friends was a smaller category of the domain *friends,* which included playmates joined together for specific purposes, little friends, and those children voluntarily selected as friends. Patrick and Bruce (Joseph) were friends, a relationship that implied certain obligations, but they were not best friends. Patrick explained, "No, he's [Bruce] just my buddy." Thus this category was perhaps best represented as a residual one for those children whose relationship never developed beyond the gradation of *friend.*

Family

Michele (Joseph) explained the differences between family and friends.

Michele She's [her best friend, Maria] kinda better than my brother and my other friend, Joey. . . . I like her better than my brother 'cause my brother goes off and plays with Joey.

Inv. Do you love Maria like your brother?

Michele No . . . because she's [Maria] not my sister or my brother or my mother or my father, so why should I love her more?

Although friends were at times strongly liked, expressions of love were stated openly by the children for family members only. This was the defining feature of this category, and a child's most intense emotional investments were reserved exclusively for family. Parents, brothers, sisters, and cousins were categorized as *friends* because they played with the children at one time or another.

A comparative analysis of the categories presented in Table 6.2 will simplify matters.

RANKING

All of the children typically engaged in ranking their friends. This not only affected the internal structure of certain categories (see Table 6.1) but also served to differentiate gradations of friendship. An example of the former is explained by Todd (Lawrence): "There's better friends, and then there's better, better friends, and then there's best, best, best friends." Richard preferred to use the word *real* as a modifier: "Andy is my real, real best friend." Although several styles existed, all of the children participated in the common practice of ranking friends (Corsaro, 1985).

Such expressions as "just my buddy" suggested that these children's friendships possessed a dimension of salience. The children were aware of different gradations of friendship and adjusted their behavior accordingly. Joshua (Lawrence) possessed a bag of 'money' during playtime that, at first, he refused to share with Todd and Alf. During the incident, he commented on his friendships with the two boys involved: "He's [Todd] just a friend friend, he's a little friend. I like Alf the best." Joshua rejected Todd's request for 'money' and shared only with Alf. Todd had mutual feelings toward Joshua: "I don't really like him much. He's just a friend."

Table 6.2 Comparison of Distinguishing Attributes of "Friends"

	Physical Contact	*Romantic*	*Availability*	*Affection (love)*	*Rank*	*Playmates*	*Authority*
Friends							
Girl	Y	Y	Y	N	N	Y	N
Boy	Y	Y	N	Y	N	Y	N
Best	Y	N	Y	N	Y	Y	N
Good	N	N	Y	N	N	Y	N
Favorite	Y	N	Y	N	N	Y	N
Friend	Y	N	Y	N	Y	Y	N
Family							
Brothers	Y	N	N	Y	N	Y	N
Sisters	Y	N	N	Y	N	Y	N
Parents	Y	N	N	Y	N	Y	Y
Cousins	Y	N	N	N	N	Y	N
Teachers							
Teachers/Principal	Y	N	N	N	N	Y	Y
School	N	N	N	N	N	N	Y

Ranking appeared to have a single function: It identified the degree of friendship and served to distinguish linguistically cherished best friends from the reservoir of classmates who occasionally received the label "friend." Best friends were distinguished by the following criteria: (a) likability, which was influenced by sharing and cooperative behavior and usually was defined in terms of niceness; (b) availability, which at school was expressed by play privileges; and (c) familiarity, which was defined by the number of play experiences (e.g., "No, he's just a friend. I only played with him twice.") and the strength of the bond.

THE CHILDREN'S USE OF FRIEND TERMS

The children employed friend terms frequently and spontaneously in casual speech. Several aspects of the labeling process are worthy of mention because these affect the friendship terms the children bestow on their classmates.

1. *Friendship terms do not denote gender or race.* Thus the children found it necessary to clarify whether I meant boy or girl friends or friends of color in my inquiries. For example, I asked Stefan (Bryant) about his friend Jack. He replied, "He's my friend in the other kindergarten, and he's brown, not like Jack in our class." The kinship term *cousin* was treated in a similar manner: "I got two boy cousins and one girl cousin."

2. *The label "friend" is given and taken away abruptly* (Jacobsen, 1975). The children were instantaneous with their anger and forgiveness. Unlike adults, there was no need to resolve conflicts with apologies. The label "friend" was retracted because of an unwillingness to share, quarrels, meanness, or failure to fulfill friend obligations. The label usually was reinstated within minutes of the offending act (see also Corsaro, 1985).

3. *Labels change.* The transition from friend to best friend was accompanied by a change in labels. This also occurred with the boyfriend/girlfriend relationship.

4. *"Romantic" interests precluded the use of the unmodified term "friend."* Once a child was considered 'romantically,' he or she received the label "boyfriend/girlfriend" consistently. Kelly (Lawrence) explained, "He's not my friend, he's my boyfriend." However, choices were often unilateral and unbeknownst to one of the children supposedly involved. This was unimportant; all that mattered was that the children considered another child as such.

5. *The children were often quite particular about their friend choices.* In fact, denial of a relationship often caused visible tension between the children involved. One morning when I was eliciting names of friends from Patrick and John (Lawrence), Patrick remarked, "Erase John, he's not my friend." John insisted he was Patrick's best friend, but Patrick emphatically denied their friendship. John was angry and hurt. By playtime, later that morning, the incident was forgotten and they were inseparable once again.

THE RULES OF FRIENDSHIP

After observing the children for several months, patterns of behavior began to emerge between children who selected each other as friends. These patterns were reduced to rules of social relationships (e.g., Argyle & Henderson, 1984; Argyle, Henderson, & Furnham, 1985; Holmes, 1990) and were correlated with linguistic data. Rules of friendship for the children included (a) sharing; (b) playing with each other; (c) showing a genuine concern for each other; (d) the acceptable use of friendship as a bartering strategy for personal gain (e.g., Schwartzman, 1978); and (e) the dissolution of a friend relationship because of a child's greediness, stinginess, or meanness (see also Corsaro, 1985; Deegan, 1991).

RACIAL RELATIONSHIPS: MAKING A FRIEND

Friendship is a meaningful part of the children's lives, for it is an expression of their social identity outside familial connections. As Corsaro (1985) suggested, these friendships are delicately conjoined with their desire to play and success at playing.

It is worthy of mention that these children's friendships were voluntary relationships (e.g., Rubin, 1980). All of the children enjoyed the freedom of entering into new relationships, maintaining favorable ones, or terminating undesirable ones. Most important, the friend relationship implied a set of obligations and expectations (e.g., Berndt & Hoyle, 1985; Selman, 1990). This knowledge was manipulated by individual bond participants but collectively shared by the children as a group.

Most of the children made friends easily and effortlessly. There was no acquaintance period or gradual exchange of personal information that is common in adult friendships. The children were concerned with the present, which for them constituted playing together (e.g., Rubin, 1980; Selman, 1980).

In the children's eyes, the process of making a friend was almost instantaneous. Prior knowledge of names was the consummate guideline for making a friend. Kevin (Lawrence) described the sequence: "Friends have to meet first. Then you introduce yourself, then they in turn say their name, then you're friends." Ken (Concord) told me his way of making a friend: "You shake his hand, then he shakes yours." Chris (Thoreau), a European American boy, made friends this way: "First you have to know his name. Then you have to find out if they're good or bad. You don't want to get into trouble. Then you have to know his name. Then you ask him to play." This was true initially, but what transpired between the process of making a friend and becoming a friend was a bit more complex than the children conceded.

Although Gottman (1983) identified social processes derived from children's conversations to explain how children become friends, the following is a descriptive and temporal account compiled from observations of classroom behavior. It describes the development of a same-sex, interracial friendship (see also Hewitt's [1986] work for a discussion of adolescent interracial friendships).

Catherine (Joseph), an African American girl, and Lauren, a European American girl, were strangers at the beginning of the school year. During the first month, these two children often communicated through gestures and pointed at one another until their names were no longer a mystery. Catherine and Lauren sat at the same table in adjacent seats.

During this critical period, Catherine and Lauren exhibited a willingness to play together. Their behavior was often cooperative, and their early associations were pleasant and favorable. Within 2 months, Catherine and Lauren had formed a stable relationship. Their actions were no longer confined to playtimes, and they frequently engaged in eye contact and conversation during classtimes. They inquired about playing at each other's houses and received invitations to each other's birthday parties.

At the end of the third month of school, Catherine and Lauren's relationship was very congenial. They were indeed friends, and I could confirm their choices by behavioral criteria. They shared snacks and toys and were genuinely concerned about one another. With predictive success, I knew a playgroup with Lauren always had Catherine by her side. Physical contact was common, and these girls were very affectionate, as the boys were with their friends. Catherine and Lauren embraced each other frequently; this behavior was intolerable from other classmates who were not friends.

At this point, a change in intensity occurred within their relationship. Catherine and Lauren were inseparable, and they now referred to one another as "best friends." They played house together constantly and took extreme measures to stand next to each other during class activities. These girls enjoyed a loyal and stable relationship clearly distinguishable from that of friends (e.g., Berndt & Hoyle, 1985; Hallinan & Teixeira, 1987).

When I asked Catherine why Lauren was her best friend, Catherine replied, "I just like her. We play house together, and we go over to each other's house. She's the bestest" (see Figure 6.1).

Forming Friendships

The first month of school was a critical period in which the children formed initial associations with their classmates. The formation of these voluntary relationships was influenced by factors related to interpersonal

Figure 6.1. Interracial best friends.

attraction for the children, such as (a) cooperative behavior (e.g., LaGaipa, 1977; Leary, Rogers, Canfield, & Coe, 1986), (b) propinquity (Hays, 1985), (c) favorable or pleasant experiences with another child (Cook, 1985; Sigelman & Welch, 1993), and (d) personality factors. Shier children remained passive during this exploratory period and made no attempt at integration.

Once a friend relationship was established, friends had to fulfill certain obligations and expectations. Failure to comply often led to the verbal termination of the relationship. But the development of the friendship bond was based on the ability of its participants to adhere to the rules.

This relationship should not be confused with the spontaneous declaration of friendship that occurred with the desire to play with a specific toy.

As the year progressed, gradations of the friendship bond emerged. The intensity and quality of friendly interaction increased with time. This change in intensity was often accompanied by a change in label from "friend" to "best friend." There was no difference in behavior between intraracial and interracial friendships (e.g., Hallinan & Teixeira, 1987; Hewitt, 1986). The participants in these relationships either complied with the expectations of how friends should behave or suffered the fate of terminating their relationship. No child was treated differently within a friendship bond because of his or her racial or ethnic membership.

Surprisingly, friendship choices remained relatively stable throughout the year (e.g., Berndt & Hoyle, 1985). However, one significant gender difference emerged concerning the maintenance of the friendship bond. The boys enjoyed stable and intensified friendships, and their loyalty was unsurpassed. By contrast, the girls' groups were extremely unstable. The loyalty so valued for boys was not at all true for the girls (e.g., Eder & Hallinan, 1978).

The quartet of Sharon, Alyssa, Michele, and Ann (Joseph) was representative. This group experienced swift changes of intensity, with short-lived dyad relationships forming between group members throughout the year. Although the group retained its integrity, there was a recurrent restructuring of dyad relationships between members. Several other girls' groups exhibited the same behavior. This was never observed with the boys.

FRIEND SELECTION

The children described the process of selecting friends as a random event, such as the phrase "you just pick them" suggests. Nevertheless, the children were emphatic and defensive about their friendship choices. Although they were not always capable of explaining the governing principles, several factors influenced their decisions.

The Notion of Similarity. Friends were chosen because they shared similar interests—for example, playing baseball. This supports the findings of social psychological literature on adult relationships and the importance of similarity in friend selection (e.g., Brehm, 1985; Drewry & Clark, 1984; Newcomb, 1961). Children apparently use the same selection processes as adults.

Although the children possessed a focal image of a friend as a child similar to themselves, race was never a factor in selecting who would or would not become a friend (see, e.g., Deegan, 1991, 1993; Hewitt, 1986). Jessie (Concord), an African American boy, and Nico, a European American boy, were friends. In deciding where to sit, Nico said, "Jessie, you're my friend." Nico put his arm around Jessie's shoulder and guided him to sit in the chair next to his. Joseph (Lawrence), an African American boy, was best friends with Michael, a European American boy. Joseph told me, "He's my best, best, best, best friend." I asked, "Why?" Joseph replied, "'Cause he lets me play at his house, and I'm going to his tree house." Not one of the children interviewed believed that friends had to share the same skin color. I asked Matt (Concord), "Do friends have to be the same color?" He replied, "No, me and Henry gots different color hands and we're friends."

A related issue is how the children treated their friends on the basis of racial or ethnic background. The following conversation occurred between Tommy (Joseph), a European American boy, and me at our table during snacktime.

Inv. Do you treat brown friends and white friends differently?

Tommy No, they're the same. Brown or white, it doesn't matter. I treat them the same. I treat them nice.

A similar response to the same question was given by Margaret (Thoreau), a European American girl. She replied, "Brown and white, they're both the same. My mommy's got whiter skin than me. She plays with me just like a friend, so I treat everybody the same."

A majority of the children responded to this question similarly, and their behavior at school toward their friends supported their answers. They did indeed show no difference in the way they treated their classmates on the basis of race or ethnicity. This is, I think, because of the children's notions of how friends should behave toward one another and the process by which they select friends. If a child were 'bad' or 'mean,' this would have precluded him or her from being chosen as a friend, and a child's race was not a factor in this decision-making process. Deegan (1991, 1993) reported similar findings with older children, so it seems reasonable to suppose that friend selection processes for children remain relatively stable and that race does not become an issue until the latter elementary or middle school years.

Also, some children mentioned that brown and white friends were treated the same because "they all have noses and ears." Thus the children used anatomical similarities that all human beings share as a guideline for how a person should be treated regardless of that person's racial or ethnic background (e.g., Wilder, 1986). Finally, some children were able to draw on their personal life experiences of being born to parents who belonged to different ethnic groups. I never witnessed an incident in which children refused to play with another child because he or she belonged to a particular racial or ethnic group.

It is worthy of reiteration that several children stated, regrettably, they would not treat friends of different ethnic groups similarly. For example, to the question, "Would you treat a white friend and a brown friend the same?" Jamie (Thoreau), a European American girl, replied, "No, 'cause they're not the same. One's got brown skin, and the other's got white skin. I got white skin too." However, because a child's response could be subjected to opposing interpretations (e.g., the desire to focus on superficial characteristics or a prejudiced attitude), the children's statements were either confirmed or refuted with ethnographic data. The real question is whether these young children treated ingroup and outgroup members differently. In general, the children's behavior confirmed that racial harmony was maintained among these 5-year-olds.

Personality/Likability. A common response to queries of friend selection was, "'Cause I just like him." Friends always were described as "nice," and a child was not chosen as a friend if he or she was too shy or bossy. Children who were mean or did not share were not likely to be selected as a friend. Sociable and cooperative children, regardless of their racial or ethnic membership, were likely to be popular in class and to have many intra- and interracial friend relations (e.g., Deegan, 1991, 1993; Hallinan & Smith, 1985; Hallinan & Teixeira, 1987; Hewitt, 1986; Leary et al., 1986).

Morality. The antithetical pair good/bad often referred to guidelines of proper behavior enforced by adults. The children wished to please; thus they chose 'those who are good' as friends. Children who "say bad words" or "push people around" were never selected.

Proximity. Propinquity played a major role in the initial establishment of friendships (Hays, 1985; Newcomb, 1981). At school, this referred to seat locations (e.g., Gump, 1978; Rizzo, 1989). As mentioned in Chapter 3, the physical arrangement of the classroom may help in fostering interracial friendships because proximity plays a prominent role in establishing relationships at school (e.g., Epstein & Karweit, 1983).

Familiarity. A stranger, which to the children meant an unfamiliar adult, was never selected as a friend. This behavior revealed the children's knowledge of social distance (see e.g., Hall, 1959; Holmes, 1992a). The children never considered an unfamiliar peer to be a stranger. This is perhaps important to the concern of parents and school personnel in educating children against the dangers of interacting with an unfamiliar adult. Finally, familiar individuals were often perceived as safe and hence more likable (Bornstein, 1989).

Behavior. Friend selection was affected by the children's behavior, such as their inability to share, or vocal qualities, such as their style of speech. Gretchen (Concord) would not choose Ian as a friend because he was "too mean" (e.g., Leary et al., 1986).

For these 5-year-old children, all of the factors that affected their choice of who would or would not become a friend had little, if any, connection to a child's racial or ethnic group membership. Young children's behavior is guided by a desire to please adults (e.g., Gesell & Ilg, 1946; Kagan, 1984; Kohlberg, 1976; Konner, 1991) and the children's notions of what it means to be a friend. Thus a child's behavior, personality, or social skills, rather than racial or ethnic heritage, were likely to determine whether he or she would form friendships.

THE GIRLFRIEND-BOYFRIEND RELATIONSHIP

"Romantic" relationships were popular topics of discussion among the children in all of the classrooms. These relationships were best described as fantasies that never materialized, rather than as actual relationships between two children of the opposite sex. This fact did not, however, diminish their significance as a type of friend relationship for these children.

By and large, "girlfriends" were more popular with the boys in all of the schools than vice versa. Sometimes the boys were preoccupied with the subject, and numerous conversations in Concord, Joseph, and Lawrence Schools centered around potential marriage partners. This was the one area in which data from the schools differed. The children from Bryant and Thoreau Schools never discussed marriage, although they did speak openly about girlfriends and boyfriends. Michael was quite fond of Mare: "She's my girlfriend. I'm going to marry her tonight." I inquired whether Mare was aware of his intentions. He blushed scarlet red, and his eyes twinkled. I am sure Mare had no idea.

All of the children discussed romantic relationships openly and teased each other publicly. Ryan (Lawrence) and John teased Roger about kissing Jane on the lips, rather than on the cheek. Outbursts such as, "Hey [boy's name], looks like you have a girlfriend," were common. This usually led to a unison chant of the love-and-marriage rhyme. Stefan (Bryant) was quick to pass along gossip to his classmates and me about the newest romantic developments. One day while he was drawing for me, Stefan remarked, "You know Ian, right? Well, now he's going with Judy."

But although some information was public knowledge, the children were quite private about their feelings. Rarely, if ever, did the children disclose such choices to classmates of their own sex. In fact, they took every precaution to ensure secrecy. Although the boys did appear to be more interested in having girlfriends, they were more embarrassed by this relationship than the girls. I suppose that is part of the reason why the boys were adamant about disclosing their girlfriend choices to other male classmates. I was honored when they trusted me as a confidante.

It was striking that children of both sexes were uninhibited about revealing their feelings in the presence of the opposite sex. I suspect that the fear of being ridiculed was stronger with same-sex companions.

The boyfriend-girlfriend relationship also was characterized by an emotional intensity not present in cross-sex friendships. The children were bashful and embarrassed whenever the subject was mentioned. Most of the children found it very difficult to conceal their feelings. Michael blushed whenever he heard Mare's name. He went to great lengths to receive her attention. He saved seats for her, gave her precious supplies, and fought to sit next to her during class activities. Dylan (Thoreau) sometimes held Gretchen's hand when they ran on the playground, but he denied emphatically that he had done so when asked by his friend Craig. Finally, cross-sex friendships appeared in greater frequency in Bryant, Lawrence, and Thoreau Schools. In these classes, the children sat either at cross-sex tables or in individual seats where children of different sexes were in close proximity. In contrast to cross-sex friendships, romantic relationships were not affected by seating patterns.

Nevertheless, this particular relationship was unlike any other because there were no obligations or expectations. But one activity was mentioned by all of the children that distinguished girlfriends-boyfriends from other peer relationships: kissing. James (Thoreau) told me about one particular bus ride he and his girlfriend shared: "I have a girlfriend, and she kissed me once on the bus. Wanna know who else I kissed?" Ryan (Joseph) went so far as to define *girlfriends* in terms of use: "Girlfriends are for kissing."

But this same activity was stripped of all meaning when the context and the participants of the situation were altered. This was never clearer than in a pair of incidents involving Trevor (Concord) and Michael (Lawrence). I was sitting at the back of the room when Trevor kissed me on the cheek in full view of his classmates. Because I was not a potential girlfriend, Trevor was unembarrassed, and no one commented on the incident. Similarly, Michael was openly affectionate with his older sister. He was unashamed when she kissed him on the lips in front of his classmates.

Choosing a Girlfriend/Boyfriend

The transition from girl to girlfriend seemed almost random at first, but closer inspection revealed distinctive qualities of choice. First and foremost, this relationship was characteristically one of physical attraction (e.g., Baron & Bryne, 1991; Dion, 1980). Girlfriends were synonymous with beauty. Todd (Lawrence) stated, "Girlfriends are pretty, prettier than just a girl in class." This dichotomy between girls in class/girls outside class had no bearing on their choices. All of the boys agreed that *their* girlfriend was the prettiest, but they did not agree on a standard of physical attractiveness. In addition to physical beauty was the factor of likability, which also plays a role in choosing a friend. A girlfriend was never a child one didn't like.

The influence of race on the children's process of selecting a potential 'romantic partner' emerged during a conversation I had with Amy (Concord), a European American girl. I must confess I was quite stunned by some of the children's thinking on who was or was not an acceptable choice for a girlfriend or boyfriend. Although interracial relationships were acceptable for children who considered each other friends, race became a criterion of selection when the relationship contained a 'romantic' element. Some of the children believed strongly that girlfriends and boyfriends should have the same color skin. Excerpts to illustrate the children's thinking on these matters appear below.

First was the issue of how children's racial membership affected their conceptions of physical attractiveness. Marty (Joseph), an African American boy, once told me, "Michele [a European American girl] is my girlfriend, and we're gonna get married today." I found this statement puzzling because these two children were often antagonistic toward one another but even more so since Marty had confided in me that he could have no girlfriends in class " 'cause all the white girls are ugly. I wish I could get big like seven so I could get a girlfriend. Randi is really my girlfriend. I need somebody that's black." Bobby (Thoreau), a Latino boy, would never choose a white girl as a girlfriend because "white girls are ugly" (e.g., see Murstein, Merighi, & Malloy, 1989, for a discussion of physical attractiveness in interracial dating). Physical attractiveness for these young children may be linked with cultural perceptions of beauty and how they perceive or feel about their 'partner' (e.g., Dion, 1986; Murstein, 1986).

Second was the factor of how the children's own racial membership influenced their selection of girlfriends/boyfriends. Some children used race as an exclusive criterion by which they selected partners. Amy's (Concord) response to the query, "What boy in class would you pick as a boyfriend?" was exemplary. She replied, "Boyfriends should be the same color as a girlfriend. Jessie gots black skin, and Nico gots white skin because they're different. But that's okay 'cause Jessie and Nico—he's friends with him. Friends can be different colors. Only if they're the same color skin for boy and girl friends." Amy would never choose Jessie as a boyfriend "because he's black."

Boys had similar feelings about their partners. The following conversation occurred between David (Joseph), a European American boy, and me during playtime.

Inv. What girls in class would you pick as a girlfriend?

David Linda and Erica and Summer.

Inv. Why did you pick them?

David Because I'm white, and they should have a white person, that's why.

Inv. Could they have a black boyfriend?

David If they wanted to they could have a black boyfriend. Some people do.

Inv. Do you mind if you see a white and a black couple together?

David Yes. My, um, my aunt's daughter has a black boyfriend, and she has a baby.

Daniel (Concord), a European American boy, was not so open-minded.

Inv. Could MaryAnn [an African American girl] be a girlfriend?

Daniel No, she's not the right kind of person.

Inv. What is the right kind of person?

Daniel One like me.

In these instances, one might reasonably conclude that the children's attitudes were influenced by and learned from extracted information from adult conversations and behavior (e.g., Branch & Newcombe, 1986; Paset & Taylor, 1991; Raman, 1984), socialization experiences (Spencer, 1988), and the media, which only recently have begun to portray interracial and ethnic couples in a positive fashion (Greenberg, 1986).

Although direct observation is likely to affect the course of development for the children's racial attitudes, I would argue that the principle of similarity is also a powerful influence in determining how these children go about selecting 'romantic' partners. This principle operates in selecting friends and also appears to be influential in selecting mates (e.g., Drewry & Clark, 1984).

Third is the issue of how the children incorporate new experiences with interracial couples into their existing knowledge of romantic couples. This cognitive limitation also may account for the children's unwillingness to accept interracial couples if they only possess a concept of romantic couples as being comprised of intraracial partners (e.g., Piaget, 1965).

The above types of responses were counterbalanced by those of children who were quite comfortable with choosing a child from a different race as a girlfriend or boyfriend. Ken (Concord), a European American boy, and I had the following conversation.

Inv. Can boyfriends and girlfriends be different colors?
Ken Yeah.
Inv. Would you ever choose a brown or black girlfriend?
Ken Yeah.
Inv. How would you feel about her?
Ken. Good. She would be pretty.

Will (Thoreau), the child of interracial parents, was asked, "Can boyfriends and girlfriends be different colors?" Will replied, "Sure. That's like in my house. One of my parents is white, and one is black. See that house across the street? One of the parents is Chinese and one is American" (see Stephan & Stephan, 1991, for an introduction on children of interracial marriages).

In an unusual occurrence, Evan (Joseph), an African American boy, asked me to help him write a love letter to Linda, a European American girl. He was very secretive about the task and asked me to move to an end table so that he could have some privacy. He was very embarrassed and did not want his fellow male classmates to see him. He delivered the letter to her desk in the presence of female classmates and did not seem to mind whether they were present when the letter was read. Because I could read, Evan asked whether I would read the note to Linda for him, which I did. Although her response was rather unemotional, he took the note and put it in her knapsack so that she could take it home. John, a European American boy, was nearby and witnessed Evan's actions. This prompted John to say, "Hey, Evan. Is she your new girlfriend?" In this case, John's response suggested that he, too, had no difficulty in accepting interracial romantic couples.

Children who had positive experiences with interracial relationships seemed quite willing to enter into them. For these children, it is possible that the principle of similarity is not so forceful a factor because it is attenuated by the children's home experiences (e.g., Spencer, 1988; Stephan & Stephan, 1991). Thus these children not only are able to compare themselves against their classmates but also are more willing to accept the differences and look past them.

It seems reasonable to conclude that these young children did not use race as a criterion with which to exclude their peers from becoming friends. Rather, it appears as though race becomes an important issue for them when they are selecting girlfriends or boyfriends. The result in some instances is the emergence of prejudiced attitudes. In the latter case, it seems likely that the children are extracting their own interpretations from adult conversations and behavior, media portrayals, and socialization experiences. This explanation appears to be logical because the children seem uninfluenced by race when selecting a same-sex friend.

Although there are arguably numerous interpretations about why some young children find interracial romantic relationships unacceptable, the one that appears to surface from this work stems from extraneous variables, such as overheard adult conversations, observations of adult role models, media influences, and the meaning children extract from these encounters. In the last case, children are attempting to accommodate the novel experience of an interracial romantic couple with their existing knowledge of this dyad. Thus one might conclude, tentatively, that adult role models who respond positively to children's questions about interracial relationships would decrease children's negative attitudes and unwillingness to select a romantic interest who was not similar to themselves (e.g., Billings, 1992).

7

Procreation and Race

The following conversation between Brian, an African American boy, Kelly, a European American girl, and me occurred in the school's (Lawrence) main corridor while the children were waiting for the afternoon school bus to arrive.

Brian [to Inv.] You're my mommy.

Inv. Could I be your mommy? [Brian nods affirmatively.]

Kelly She's my mommy. She can't be yours. Your mommy's black 'cause you're black.

Brian Well, my hair's black, and Mrs. Holmes's hair is black, so she could be my mommy too.

Kelly was convinced that Brian's mother must have a skin color similar to his. Apparently, her notion of similarity extended to include parental resemblance. Brian was clearly less concerned with phenotypic skin color. He simply wanted to call the investigator his mommy. To do so, he extended the principle of similarity to include hair color. In this instance, the children involved were jovial because they knew they were pretending, and their behavior suggested that they had a sense of procreational similarity after all. This incident serves as an introduction to the influence that color and race have on the children's notions of sexual reproduction.

The relationship between the children's notions of procreation and their knowledge of race and, consequently, color is explored in the following areas: (a) the biological process of childbirth and (b) how the children's knowledge of reproduction influences their cognitive notions of parent-child resemblance. These areas are not mutually exclusive; rather, they possess overlapping boundaries (e.g., Anderson, 1975; Kempton, 1978; Rosch, 1973).

CHILDBIRTH AND PROCREATION

The topic of childbirth was a salient one for the children and often arose spontaneously in casual conversation among them. This frequency stems, in part, from the fact that during the research, 18 of the kindergarten children experienced the arrival of a new sibling. Thus most of the children were exposed indirectly to or experienced personally the unfolding of this biological process.

At first, it appeared that the children had a simplistic and inaccurate view of childbirth. This was attributed initially to limitations in their cognitive abilities at this age (e.g., Gesell & Ilg, 1946; Kagan, 1984; Piaget, 1963) and their interpretations of explanations they acquired from parents, caretakers, older siblings, and peers.

Of the 102 children, 95 concurred with a statement made by Mare (Thoreau), an African American girl: "Babies come from their mother's stomach. I came from my mother's tummy." One day after arriving in class, I was met by Sharon (Lawrence), a European American girl, who announced proudly, "Robyn, my mommy's tummy is getting bigger and bigger and bigger. She better have the baby soon or else she's gonna explode. She has to go to the hospital soon, but I get to stay over my grandma's house." No child believed that babies come from their mother's belly button—a characteristic response for children around 3 years of age (e.g., Gesell & Ilg, 1946).

Although nearly all the children believed that 'babies come from their mothers' bellies,' there also existed an extreme range of interindividual variation regarding the children's knowledge of childbirth. Some children believed only in the notion that a baby came from his or her mother's belly. Other children held several beliefs that existed together with the former notion. Seven children confessed they did not know how babies were born. When I asked Terri (Bryant), an African American girl, "How are babies born?" she replied, "I never knew that." Still other children responded surprisingly with elaborate and accurate descriptions of childbirth. The children's responses on the subject of childbirth appear in Table 7.1.

The following examples illustrate the range of knowledge the children shared on childbirth as individual members of a childhood culture. Mare and Jake (Thoreau), two African American children, were drawing pic-

Table 7.1 The Children's Conceptions of Childbirth

School	*Race/ Ethnicity*	*Baby Comes From Mother's Belly*	*No Knowledge*	*Father Does Not Take Part*
Bryant	Af Am	15	2	10
	Euro Am	3	—	1
	Latino	4	—	3
	Other	1	—	—
Concord	Af Am	4	—	1
	Euro Am	13	—	10
	Latino	2	—	1
	Other	2	1	—
Joseph	Af Am	8	1	7
	Euro Am	6	—	3
	Latino	2	—	1
Lawrence	Af Am	2	—	1
	Euro Am	15	2	12
	Latino	1	—	1
	Other	1	—	—
Thoreau	Af Am	15	—	11
	Euro Am	4	1	1
	Latino	3	—	2

tures for me of Mommy having a baby, when the following conversation occurred.

Jake Draw a man for me.
Mare [to Jake] A man can't have a baby.
Inv. How does Mommy have a baby?
Mare I'll tell you in your ear. Keep it a secret, okay?

(She begins to whisper, but I was distracted by the background noise at playtime.)

Inv. . . . Could you tell me in my ear again? I won't tell anyone.
Mare Jake's gonna hear it. Could we go over there?

Figure 7.1. Mommy having a baby.

(Mare pulls the investigator to the classroom door. The conversation is no longer audible to Jake. In the private area, Mare whispers this in my ear. See Figure 7.1.)

Later during the same drawing session, Anne (Thoreau), an African American girl, conveyed to me the following information on childbirth.

Anne Mommy's happy 'cause she's having a baby.

Inv. How does Mommy have a baby?

Anne Well, first she gets married, and then the egg is very little, and then as soon as it gets bigger it hatches. And then there's the baby, and you go to the hospital and then you get the baby tooken out.

Inv. Where does the baby come out?

Anne Your stomach.

Inv. Exactly where, please point for me.

Anne [Points to a spot right near the start of the rib cage]

Mare [seated nearby, interjects] Uh, uh. I'll tell her. I could only tell the girls. [Jake and Jimmy were present, so Mare whispered in Anne's ear.]

Anne Aah! [Simultaneously covering her mouth with the palm of her hand]

Alyssa (Joseph), an African American girl, provided some additional information for me (see Figure 7.2).

Inv. How are babies born?

Alyssa First they [mothers] have it [the baby] in their stomach, and then they go the hospital, and then they have to lay down, and then for the baby to come out they have to push. And, um, there it comes.

Finally, Stefan (Bryant), an African American boy, gave a description of childbirth that deserves mention.

Inv. How do you think babies are born?

Steven In the stomach.

Inv. How does the baby come out?

Steven You gotta open it (the stomach) up.

Inv. How would you open it up?

Steven You gotta open it up with your hands. [As he speaks, he simultaneously gestures. His fingertips are touching right below the start of his rib cage. He mimics pulling the skin apart and pulls his hands across his chest as if opening it up from the center of the body to the sides.] You gotta put gloves on to take the baby out, and then you gotta wipe all the red stuff off the baby.

One might conclude that this young boy is describing his interpretation of a cesarean delivery. The importance of the children's interpretation of everyday events and the meaning they extract from adult behavior has

Figure 7.2. Mommy having a baby in the hospital.

emerged throughout this text (e.g., Aboud, 1988; Raman, 1984; Turner & Bruner, 1986).

The above conversations illustrate two important aspects of the children's knowledge of procreation: (a) It is acquired and synthesized from experiential learning and interpretations of information and explanations from those individuals who come in contact with the children, and (b) girls are more accurate than boys in describing this process. For example, girls were more likely to include such terms as *private area, hospital, push,* and *lay down* in their descriptions of childbirth. Boys responded typically to the query, "How do you think babies are born?" with "in the stomach."

In addition, conversations involving certain anatomical references were taboo and were carried on only in the presence of one's own sex. Thus, in the episode with Mare and Jake (Thoreau), Jake was excluded from the conversation because of his sex, and Anne and I were allowed to participate because of ours. Sexual cleavage at this age is influenced also by reinforcement at school ("good girl"), the children's play behavior (e.g., Ignico, 1990; Maccoby & Jacklin, 1987; Sutton-Smith, 1979), and the children's self-definitions and conceptions (e.g., Kagan, 1984).

Finally, 33 European American children, 30 African American children, and 8 Latino children did not recognize the part the father played in conception. For these children, the mother was responsible exclusively for the child's existence and for giving birth to the baby. The importance of this belief emerges in the children's understanding of the relationship between parent-child resemblances and phenotypic traits such as skin color.

MOMMY AND THE COLOR OF THE BABY

To determine the children's knowledge of procreation and how this was affected by the race and color of one's parents, two strategies were employed: (a) informal interviewing while the children were drawing and (b) the presentation of a series of pictures of parents of various skin colors. The second method requires explanation.

The children were presented individually with four pictures arranged in the same sequence for all subjects. The order of the pictures was (a) a European American heterosexual couple, (b) an African American heterosexual couple, (c) a Latino heterosexual couple, and (d) an African American woman holding a European American baby on her lap.

All of the children then were asked the same set of questions (phrased initially in the singular and then, during the second trial, in the plural) about the pictures. This procedure was repeated 1 month later. The questions corresponded to the order of the pictures and were delivered to the children as follows. "Here is a mommy and daddy. What color baby do you think they have?" or "Here are mommies and daddies. What color

Table 7.2 The Effect of Skin Color on the Children's Notions of Procreation

School	*Race/ Ethnicity*	*Mother/Child Same Color*	*Parent/Child Same Color*	*Parents Must Be Same Color*
Bryant	Af Am	13	6	8
	Euro Am	3	2	1
	Latino	2	2	—
Concord	Af Am	2	3	2
	Euro Am	13	11	13
	Latino	1	2	1
Joseph	Af Am	11	6	8
	Euro Am	6	5	5
	Latino	1	3	1
Lawrence	Af Am	2	1	2
	Euro Am	15	9	15
	Latino	1	—	1
Thoreau	Af Am	13	5	10
	Euro Am	3	3	6
	Latino	1	1	1

children do you think they have?" These questions were repeated for the first three pictures. The question, "Here is a mommy with her baby. How do you think she had this baby?" pertained exclusively to the fourth picture. The children's notion of procreation and how it is affected by race is presented in Table 7.2.

Children of Homogeneous Racial/Ethnic Parents

One of the most important factors that affected how these children linked procreation with skin color and parent-child resemblance was their knowledge of childbirth. Most of the children who believed that "babies come from their mommy's tummy" also inferred that the mother alone must be responsible for the baby's skin color.[1] For them, skin color was an inherited trait transmitted from mother to child in an unaltered state. Jason (Joseph), a European American boy, made the following deduction about the connection between a mother and the future skin color of her children:

Inv. These are mommies and daddies. What color do you think their children are?

Jason Babies come from their mommy's tummy. My mommy just had a baby, so they're the same color as their mommy.

Similarly, the investigator asked Bruce (Lawrence), a Latino boy:

Inv. Do you think I could have a brown baby?

Bruce Nope.

Inv. Why not?

Bruce 'Cause you're white.

Molly (Thoreau), a European American girl, explained it to me in the following manner.

Inv. Here are mommies and daddies. What color do you think their children are?

Molly Mommies and daddies have kids their same color because the baby has to be the same color as the mommy.

When I asked the children what color they thought my own parents were, almost all responded with "white," and there was little, if any, variation between children of different racial and ethnic groups. Of the African American and Latino children, 21 and 8, respectively, believed in the notion that parental resemblance must extend to skin color (see Table 7.2). For example, consider a dialogue between Jack (Bryant), an African American boy, and me.

Inv. Here are a mommy and a daddy [white couple]. What color baby do you think they have?

Jack White.

Inv. Why?

Jack Because they're both white.

Although this was the prevailing view among most of the children, a child's genealogy and social exposure to interracial couples clearly influenced the children's perceptions and knowledge of the interplay between parental skin color and that of their progeny. The following dialogues illustrate several points. The first addresses the finding that children (regardless of their racial or ethnic membership) who had no exposure to interracial couples responded to the questions on skin color and procreation in predictable ways. The conversation below occurred between Martina (Lawrence), a European American girl, and me.

Inv. Do you think your parents could have a baby Ken's color [brown]?

Martina No, because my mommy and daddy have light skin. They can't 'cause they don't have the same skin color. Mommies and daddies have the same skin color as their babies.

The notion that parents and children must be the same color also extends (for some of the children) to the belief that parents themselves must be the same skin color (see Table 7.2). For example, Curt (Bryant), a European American boy, came to this conclusion:

Inv. If Mommy and Daddy had another baby, what color do you think the baby would be?

Curt Same color as my mom and dad.

Inv. Is it possible for mommies and daddies to be different colors?

Curt No.

Inv. Why not?

Curt Because everybody in our house has the same, the same skin color.

Children who believed that parents and children should have similar skin colors solved the question of how an African American (brown) woman could have a European American (white) baby by using similar strategies. A list of the children's explanations and the frequency with which they were reported appear in Table 7.3. Although the explanations vary, the reasoning employed by the children in answering the query was consistent: They believed the woman and child in the photograph were not mother and child because they had different skin colors. These children could not comprehend the possibility that children and their parents could have different skin colors.

Of the 102 children queried, 20 believed that an African American woman could have a European American baby through adoption. For example:

Inv. How do you think a mommy and baby get to be different colors?

Table 7.3 The Children's Explanations About How an African American Mother Could Have a European American Child

School	*Race/ Ethnicity*	*Adoption*	*Baby-Sitter*	*Doesn't Belong to Her*	*No Reply*
Bryant	Af Am	2	6	4	3
	Euro Am	1	1	1	—
	Latino	—	1	1	—
Concord	Af Am	1	—	2	1
	Euro Am	5	5	4	—
	Latino	1	—	1	—
Joseph	Af Am	1	5	4	4
	Euro Am	1	4	—	2
	Latino	—	1	1	—
Lawrence	Af Am	1	—	1	1
	Euro Am	3	—	5	7
	Latino	1	—	—	—
Thoreau	Af Am	2	4	1	1
	Euro Am	1	—	—	2
	Latino	1	1	—	—

Malcolm Um, 'cause they're from different tummies. Some, sometimes people don't want babies and they give them away.

Inv. You mean like in adoption?

Malcolm Black babies are adopted too.

A larger number of children—28—concluded that the African American woman simply was baby-sitting the child. For example:

Inv. How do you think this mommy had this baby?

Curt Maybe she's just baby-sitting him.

Ten boys decided the baby must not belong to the mommy. For example:

Inv. How do you think this mommy had this baby?

Chas I don't know. Maybe she's not his mommy.

Fifteen girls concluded that the baby was given to the mother and did not belong to her. For example:

Inv. How do you think this mommy had this baby?
Wilma Somebody gave it to her. They should be the same color.

Included here are the responses from three female children who believed the woman took the baby from its mother. For example:

Inv. How do you think this mommy had this baby?
Marly 'Cause she took it from his mommy.

Children who believed that parent-child resemblances must extend to skin color also acknowledged one exception: It was acceptable for parents and their children to be varying shades of the same color. This finding requires a more elaborate discussion.

Jenna (Concord), an African American girl, reveals in the subsequent section on interracial unions that parents should be the same color as their children to avoid ridicule. Yet to the query, "What color are your mommy and daddy?" Jenna responded, "Brown, but my brother and daddy are darker brown." This was a puzzling statement because it seemed inconsistent with her beliefs on how children with parents of differing colors are treated. She stated that her own brother and father were darker than she was, yet she maintained that parents and their children should be the same skin color. The incongruity in her responses can be explained as follows.

Skin color is a genetic trait controlled by multiple genes that potentially can produce great phenotypic variation, even between members of the same immediate family. Young children are responsive to and perceive observable differences between individuals, and nuance of skin color is perhaps the most salient observable characteristic that serves to attract the children's attention when comparing themselves with others (e.g., Aboud, 1987; Coles, 1964; Gesell & Ilg, 1946; Kagan, 1984; Ramsey, 1987).

Thus it seems reasonable to suppose that young children are also sensitive to and can perceive subtle variations in the same skin color (e.g., Berlin & Kay, 1991; Coles, 1964; Williams & Morland, 1976). Because children are attracted naturally to observable differences, it was not surprising that Jenna noticed and conveyed information about the different degrees of brown skin color in her family.

A similar pattern of responses emerged with the European American and Latino children even though nuances in white skin color are presumably less visible and more difficult to detect. Rachel (Thoreau), a Latino girl, and I were playing outside on the swings during the following conversation.

Inv. Do parents have to be the same skin color as their children?

Rachel Yes, they should have the same skin color.

Inv. Tell me about your mommy and daddy.

Rachel My mommy's the same color as me, but she's a little bit tanner. And my daddy's even a bit more tanner than my mommy, but he's not as tan as Derrick [a dark brown African American boy who ran past her].

Kyle (Concord), a fair-skinned European American boy, responded similarly: "My brother's kinda white, like pink. He's darker than me, and we have the same mommy."

From these examples, it appears that these children are cognizant of and accept differences in skin color between a parent and child, provided that they vary by degree within the same color category (e.g., Rosch, 1973; Rosch & Lloyd, 1978).

Nevertheless, the children recognized stark contrasts in parent-child skin colors and consequently classified them into separate color categories. The latter behavior was not inconsistent with their belief that parents must be the same color; rather, it validated the children's cognitive notions of how skin color is transmitted from parent to child.

Although the means by which children internally structure social and color categories was discussed in Chapter 4, a brief reiteration of this topic is warranted here. It is plausible that the children structured skin color categories around Rosch's (1973) notion of a focal type in which inclusive members of the category vary by degree of representativeness with respect to the most typical or focal member. This is a possible explanation for why children place family members who have the same skin color, albeit varying nuances of the same color, into the same color category, rather than into contrasting ones (e.g., see Berlin & Kay's [1991] work for a discussion of spectral color classification that identified similar principles of category formation from cross-cultural data with adults).

Children of Interracial Parents

Children who were born to interracial or interethnic couples or who had social experiences with families in which the parents had differing skin colors responded quite differently to queries of parent-child resemblances when compared with children who had parents of the same skin color. The former children offered the following as explanations for the differences in skin color between a child and his or her parents.

Inv. These are mommies and daddies. What color do you think their children are?

Mike My daddy's way darker than me, so they don't have to be the same color. [Mike (Concord) has an Arabic father and European American mother.]

Bob (Bryant) offered the following information when presented with the query concerning the link between the mother and child in the picture.

Inv. How do you think this brown mommy had this white baby?

Bob He came out of her tummy.

Inv. If his mommy's tummy is brown, how did he get to be white?

Bob 'Cause he had a white father. Jackie's brown, and he got a white father too.

The children's social experiences did indeed affect their perceptions, and this was found to supersede the race, ethnicity, and socioeconomic status of the child. Zach (Concord), a European American boy, lived in an upper-class neighborhood. Here is his response to whether a brown mommy could have a white baby.

Inv. Do you think your mommy could have a brown baby?

Zach Yeah, I was at my baby-sitter's house, and there was this mommy that's white and the baby's brown. They can be different colors.

Inv. Do you think I could have a brown or black baby?

Zach Yes. You can have a white baby or a black baby or a brown baby. They don't have to be the same color as the mom.

Finally, a large number of children (25) could not provide an answer to the question of how a brown mommy could have a white baby. These children responded with, "I don't know."

It seems reasonable to conclude that children who believe they must necessarily be the same skin color as their parents solve the query of how an African American woman could have a European American baby on the basis of their (a) limitations in cognitive abilities (e.g., Aboud & Skerry, 1984; Piaget, 1965; Spencer, 1988), (b) belief that a mother passes on her skin color in an unaltered state to her baby because the baby comes from the mother's stomach, (c) familial relationships and limited exposure to interracial couples (e.g., Spencer, 1988), and (d) ability to perceive stark differences in skin color between a parent and child while accepting subtle nuances of the same color. Prior positive social experiences and exposure to interracial couples may help eradicate some of the prejudices that exist for children born to parents of differing races or ethnic groups (e.g., see Aboud, 1988; Bunton & Weissbach, 1974; Schofield, 1986; Stephan & Stephan, 1991, for effective intervention programs in reducing prejudice in children).

THE CHILDREN'S SUBJECTIVE FEELINGS ON INTERRACIAL UNIONS

It seems appropriate, in discussing the children's notion of procreation and how it is influenced by parental skin color, to touch on the children's subjective feelings of interracial unions. Consider the following dialogue between Jenna (Concord), an African American girl, and me.

Inv. Do you think mommies and daddies should be the same color?

Jenna Yes.

Inv. Would it be all right if they were different colors?

Jenna No, 'cause if they're different colors, then everybody would laugh at you.

This kind of response was not received exclusively from African American children, for these children were more accepting of interracial relationships than either European American or Latino children were (e.g., see the article "Interracial Dating," 1993, for a discussion of African American college students' opinions on interracial dating). For example, Mark (Bryant), a European American boy, expressed similar feelings.

Inv. How would you feel if one of your parents was white and your other parent was black?

Mark Sad. People could make fun of me, and they would hurt my feelings and everybody's feelings. One time, I made fun of somebody and they said, "You hurt my feelings."

In the examples above, the children do not share membership in a common racial or ethnic group. Children who believed they would be ridiculed because their parents did not have the same skin color were influenced, in part, by

- the fact that their parents possessed the same skin complexion and the children's cognitive inabilities to accommodate novel experiences into their existing notions of what skin color parents should have (e.g., Piaget, 1965)
- social experiences and societal and parental attitudes (e.g., Phinney & Rotheram, 1987; Raman, 1984; Spencer, 1988). Although these are particularly attenuated in young children (e.g., Branch & Newcombe, 1986), they do overhear adult conversations and extract the information that is meaningful for them (see Chapter 6).
- the fact that these children probably had limited exposure to interracial couples
- the influence of the children's notion that a child must have the same skin color as his or her mother because children come from their mother's belly

A striking contrast appears in the responses of children born to interracial parents. Consider, for example, the dialogue between Caren (Bryant), who has a European American mother and African American father, and me.

Caren My dad's brown.

Inv. What color is Mommy?

Caren White.

Inv. Would you rather Mommy and Daddy be the same color?

Caren I like them different colors. Like you and Stefan are different colors, and Lynn and you are different colors.

Inv. How do you feel about having a mommy and daddy that are different colors?

Caren Like they should be nice to each other and pick up their own kids and being nice to them.

Children born to interracial parents did not mention that other people would make fun of them. They responded positively to such questions and focused on the actual relationship and duties of their parents, rather than on their skin colors. Thus these children moved away from observable differences and focused on the quality of attachment and the affective nature of the parent-child relationship (e.g., Aboud, 1988). This was in direct contrast to the opinions expressed by the majority of children who had parents of the same skin color.

Children who had social experiences with children of interracial unions also responded confidently to queries on this subject. For example, Anne, Kathy, and Ricky (Thoreau), all African American children, and I were drawing at the back table when the following conversation occurred. The children and I were discussing the possibilities of skin color for children based on the skin color of their parents.

Kathy There's brown babies and white babies.

Anne Ricky has a black mommy. [He nods yes to the group.]

Kathy So.

Anne And he's white.

Kathy And his brother's black. So.

Anne He was born like that. His brother's brown.

Ricky was totally at ease with the conversation of his classmates. Although Kathy and Anne have parents of the same skin color, the two girls did not ridicule Ricky. Rather, their exposure to and positive experiences with children of interracial couples in their neighborhoods led to their accepting and positive view of these children.

It seems fitting to end this chapter with an example of how children from interracial unions view their parents. The dialogue is a testimony to the innocence and candor that radiate from young children. Timmy (Joseph), an African American boy, and I were playing on the swings when the following conversation occurred.

Inv. Do mommies and daddies have to be the same color?

Timmy No.

Inv. Why not?

Timmy My mommy's white, and my daddy's black. What color are your mommy and daddy?

Inv. My mommy and daddy are the same color.

Timmy You mean they're not different colors?

Inv. No, they're the same color.

Timmy I like them different colors like my mommy and daddy, but it's okay, Robyn, if yours are the same color.

In summary, it appears that children's notions of childbirth, their relationship to race, and their subjective impressions about interracial adult unions are influenced by (a) cognitive abilities—the focus on affective states and perceptual differences, rather than cognition (e.g., Aboud, 1988; Kohlberg, 1976; Ramsey, 1987; Zajonc, 1980); (b) socialization experiences and interactions with different ethnic groups (e.g., Aboud & Skerry, 1984; Spencer, 1988); (c) preferences for ingroup members (Asher & Allen, 1969; Corenblum & Annis, 1987; Hunsberger, 1978); (d) the belief that skin color is a genetically transmitted trait in an unalterable form; and (e) societal attitudes (e.g., Phinney & Rotheram, 1987; Raman, 1984).

Adults should be encouraged to discuss the process of childbirth with young children. Children are naturally curious about bodily functions, and it would be easy for a teacher to integrate a simplistic presentation of childbirth into a class lesson. For example, a parent could be invited to bring an infant to class and participate in the discussion of childbirth. Early positive exposure to and interaction with children of all colors—for example, the opportunity for a kindergartner to see an African American, European American, or Latino infant—may be one effective strategy that can teach children to be accepting of all children, regardless of whether or not they or their parents are the same color.

NOTE

1. For the purpose of racial and ethnic classification at school, a child was assigned to the group of his or her mother.

8

Conclusion

When I began studying young children's social relationships, my primary concern was whether as an adult I could gain a clear and accurate view of the world through a child's eyes. After reading an overview of the existing literature, I pondered the methodological considerations. The question of how to collect the data was a crucial one because this technique would determine, almost exclusively, the richness of the information obtained from the children.

My training as an anthropologist led me to decide on participant observation (e.g., Agar, 1980; Berentzen, 1989; Fine & Sandstrom, 1988; Spradley, 1980) as my primary method of investigation. The data were supplemented with informal interviewing and the collection of children's drawings, and these strategies facilitated the ease with which I established relationships with the children and allowed us to develop a special rapport. I was an adult who played with them, had to do schoolwork, and never disciplined them. I was rewarded for these actions by receiving the children's trust and their graciousness in conversing with me about matters of race and ethnicity.

If we can agree that our children are the future and that adults are responsible for developing educational and social programs for them, then it is the children to whom we should be listening. This is best accomplished by acquiring a child's perspective on the world—through the method of participant observation.

A case in point is the solutions the children offered for attaining racial harmony in our society. I asked the children, "Why do you think some white and brown people don't get along, and how do you think we could get them to be friends?" Eddie (Thoreau), an African American boy, responded, "That's easy. Don't fight with them. No punchin' and no smacking." Meghan (Lawrence), a European American girl, had this suggestion: "You make friends with them. Then you play together, then you go to the same school, and then you can walk to school together." Michaela (Joseph), a Latino girl, responded, "Be nice to them, and like if you go to the same school, you could sit at their table and then play with them. And then you could sit down together in the lunchroom. Then you're friends." Janice (Concord), a European American girl, responded, "Show them the things you like to do and then ask them to do those things with you. Then you do what they like to do." Finally, Stefan's (Bryant) response stated the goal concisely: "Everybody gots to get along."

The children's ability and willingness to offer solutions for racial harmony reflect the general climate of racial attitudes and beliefs observed in all of the schools. Although a majority of research studies have discussed the ineffectiveness of school desegregation in reducing racial tensions and barriers (Cook, 1984; Gerard, 1983; Hawley, 1988; Katz & Taylor, 1988; Schofield, 1986), the kindergarten children of this study exhibited little animosity or prejudice toward classmates from racial and ethnic outgroups. This finding appears to be in line with developmental research suggesting that racial tensions increase generally with age (e.g., Schofield, 1989). Hence the racial cleavage that emerges in the latter elementary grades (Hallinan & Teixeira, 1987; Schofield, 1984) was not observed with these young children.

In explaining the discrepancies found among researchers examining the effectiveness of desegregation, Cook (1984) proposed that disparate interpretations may be based on the context and conditions in which the studies were conducted. Although this explanation is plausible, I believe two factors are primarily responsible for the lack of racial tension and prejudice observed among these young children; these factors are entwined with the kindergarten experience and help explain the children's willingness to enter into voluntary interracial relationships.

First is the question of whether racial integration in schools has been effective (Cook, 1984; Gerard, 1983; Katz & Taylor, 1988). Apparently, contact in itself is not sufficient to reduce prejudice, for if this were true, school desegregation should have been successful (Cook, 1984). Research evidence demonstrates that desegregation has not facilitated the breaking down of racial barriers (Katz & Taylor, 1988; Schofield, 1979, 1986; Stephan, 1978).

A majority of these studies, however, were conducted in middle schools and with older children. The racial and gender cleavage that surfaces in the later elementary school years (Maccoby, 1990; Sagar, Schofield, & Snyder, 1985) was not observed in any measurable frequency for the kindergarten children in this project. Thus a child's age and cognitive abilities may be one factor that could account for the racial harmony observed. Young children tend to identify and focus on superficial characteristics and differences among people (Aboud, 1988; Butler, 1989; Harter, 1983; Ramsey, 1987). They are not yet capable of making the psychological distinctions, succumbing to peer pressure, or recognizing the importance of similar attitudes and mores as a basis for friendship—factors that presumably are responsible for the racial and gender prejudice observed in the later elementary grades (Feingold, 1988; Hallinan & Teixeira, 1987; Maccoby, 1990; Sagar et al., 1985).

Second is the influence of a school's curriculum on the effectiveness of racial integration. The more rigid, traditional curriculum of the later elementary grades provides little opportunity for small cooperative group projects. Rather, students are confined to their seats for most of the school day, and their voluntary and cooperative interactions with peers occur during recess periods. As Aronson (1986) and Cook (1984) suggested, the failure to create cooperative, pleasant interactions in schools has hindered the development of interracial relations. Herein lies the strength of the kindergarten curriculum in improving race relations.

It has been demonstrated that the use of interracial cooperative groups in schools has positive effects on interracial attitudes and race relations (Cook, 1985; Goleman, 1989; Hollifield & Slavin, 1983; Johnson & Johnson, 1981; Minuchin & Shapiro, 1983). It seems possible that the racial harmony observed with the kindergarten children could be due, in part, to the format of the curriculum that provides positive experiences with racial outgroup members in voluntary cooperative small group projects.

Thus it is my contention that the lack of racial tensions observed with these young children from racially diverse schools was facilitated by two interactive factors: (a) the age and cognitive abilities of the children studied and (b) a school curriculum that provided ample opportunities for small cooperative group interactions that led to early positive experiences with racial outgroup members.

In this book, I have focused on young children's racial beliefs and attitudes, and important findings have emerged on this subject. Included here are (a) how the children categorize people on the basis of race and ethnicity, (b) how the children view interracial romantic relationships and why race is an issue in such relationships, (c) why race is not a factor in selecting a same-sex friend, (d) how interracial relationships develop, and (e) how children's notions of race affect their knowledge of procreation.

Two central themes are omnipresent in discussions of the children's knowledge of race and ethnicity that may have implications for educators and any other adults who interact regularly with young children (e.g., Billings, 1992; Wieseman, 1986): (a) how children form and construct their concepts and categories for people (Mervis, 1987; Rosch & Lloyd, 1978) and (b) how children incorporate new personal experiences into their notions of racial and ethnic categories (e.g., Aboud & Skerry, 1984; Piaget, 1963, 1965; Spencer, 1988).

Consider the first theme—how children form and construct their concepts and categories for people. The following anecdote reinforces the attributes and features mentioned throughout this book that young children find important in classifying people.

During one holiday season, I was standing in line to pay for my purchases at a Toys R Us store. In front of me was a European American girl, approximately 5 years of age, with a young man who was her father. Directly behind me was an older African American gentleman. The 5-year-old was beginning to lose patience and turned toward me. She said, "Hi," and then exclaimed, "Daddy, that man has real black skin."

The father of the child was terribly embarrassed by his child's outburst and apologized to the African American man. The man quickly countered with, "Yes, I do have black skin, but I'm just like you only a different color."

The point of the encounter and dialogue is that young children, as demonstrated throughout the text, tend to focus on overt or superficial characteristics when attempting to structure their categories (e.g., Aboud, 1988; Burns, 1979; Harter, 1983; Ramsey, 1987). This is particularly true when they classify people. Therefore, educators and others who interact regularly with young children should have knowledge of child developmental issues and children's cognitive abilities. Such individuals should be sensitive when they refer, in the presence of children, to certain colors as gender specific or as having pleasurable or undesirable qualities (Spencer, 1988; Williams & Morland, 1976). A common example is the association of the color black with evil or badness (e.g., Needham, 1973, 1980; Spencer, 1988).

Young children do not necessarily categorize the world in the same way adults do (e.g., Mervis, 1987), yet they are capable of recognizing similarities and differences among categories. Thus it is possible to teach children about the commonalities human beings share, as well as to appreciate the differences among us.

The second theme—how children incorporate new personal experiences into their notions of racial and ethnic categories—can be best explained in Piagetian terms. Although I disagree with Piaget's (1963, 1965) theory of cognitive development that places children neatly into stages at various ages, I do find merit in his notion that children learn and acquire knowledge by adapting to their environment. In this connection, I find his complementary terms of *assimilation* and *accommodation* especially applicable in discussing how young children develop and acquire knowledge about social cognition—in particular, race and ethnicity.[1]

Consider children who have limited or virtually no contact with members from racial or ethnic groups to which they themselves do not belong. In the process of acquiring knowledge about matters of racial identity and social cognition (Cross, 1985; Erikson, 1963; Spencer, 1985, 1988), a child must incorporate each new social encounter with existing mental schema he or she already possesses. One negative experience with an individual from a different racial group may lead a child to include the attribute of meanness in determining what it means to be a member of that racial group. (e.g., Judd & Park, 1988; Quattrone, 1986). Because of limited contact, it is possible that the child then extends this attribute to all members of the racial group. Thus one can see how stereotypical beliefs arise and could be perpetuated before children are capable of developing prejudiced attitudes (Devine, 1989). By contrast, positive interracial encounters could serve to add prosocial attributes to the child's still incomplete construction of a racial or ethnic category.

The value of providing positive interracial experiences is crucial for young children who still do not have a complete mental schema for categories of people, but who include attributes they deem relevant (e.g., Mervis, 1987). Thus the integration of small cooperative group tasks into educational curricula is valuable because research confirms that they foster positive interracial relationships (e.g., Aboud, 1988; Hallinan & Teixeira, 1987; Pettigrew, 1986; Schofield, 1993).

The same line of thought may be applied to how children conceive of and subjectively feel about interracial romantic relationships. Children born to parents of the same ethnic or racial group or to parents of differing racial and ethnic groups base their notions of who is or is not an acceptable romantic partner on their own parental bond.

Thus, when children are confronted with a romantic relationship that differs from their own experiences, they need to accommodate their new experiences with their existing notions of what constitutes a viable romantic couple. Environmental variables, such as direct observations of adult behavior (Bandura, 1977) and media influence (Comstock & Paik, 1991; Van Evra, 1990), as socializing agents may lead children to extract their own meaning from these events. This exposure, coupled with the child's need to accommodate new experiences, may or may not lead to prejudiced behaviors, depending on what information is presented. In short, children's knowledge about racial and ethnic relationships is acquired through their own active adaptations to their environments and extraneous variables, such as direct observations of adult behavior (Bandura, 1977; Raman, 1984), nonverbal cues (e.g., Hall, 1959), and the media (Comstock & Paik, 1991; Kottak, 1990; Van Evra, 1990). The importance of parental attitudes and behavior and media influence is demonstrated clearly in the children's beliefs about interracial romantic relationships.

My goal in writing this book was to present children's notions of racial and ethnic matters in their own terms. As an adult participant observer, however, I must confess that simply acting like a child does not give one the right to claim that one can learn exactly how a child conceives of such matters. As Fine and Sandstrom (1988) and Turner and Bruner (1986) suggested, however, participating in the daily activities of a child allows one to experience and feel the elements of the child's complete universe—his or her social, cognitive, emotional, and physical spheres. Through these experiences, adults as participant observers in the culture of childhood come to learn how children view the world. Working with young children is a pleasure and a privilege. It also offers the researcher the joy of revisiting the carefree, candid, and innocent times of childhood and conveying that journey to others.

NOTE

1. The terms *assimilation* and *accommodation* are defined, respectively, as a child's ability to incorporate new information into an already existing mental scheme, and a child's ability to alter an existing mental scheme to accommodate new information (e.g., Piaget, 1963).

Appendix

Sample Tape Transcription

DECEMBER 31, 1991
MORNING SESSION, CONCORD SCHOOL

J, an African American girl, is the first one to draw for me at playtime. She begins by drawing a picture of a park.

Inv. What kind of picture do you want to draw for me?

J This is a tree, um, I mean a park.

Inv. Can you please draw a picture of yourself in the park for me? [She nods yes.]

Inv. Do you think there are different kinds of people?

J [She nods yes.] Some peoples are black. Some peoples are white. And some peoples are Spanish.

Inv. What is the difference between somebody who is black and somebody who is Spanish?

J Look at the people. [She is talking about her picture.] It's my brother.

Inv. Can you tell me what is the difference between a person who is black and one who is Spanish?

J My baby-sitter is Spanish, and she talks Spanish. Spanish people have to talk Spanish.

Inv. Is there a difference between somebody who is black and somebody who is white?

J [She nods yes.]

Inv. What is the difference?

J Well, somebody's skin is white, and somebody's skin is black or brown. Some skin is white, and some is black. They're different 'cause that's the way it is. This one is black, this one is brown. [She is holding up a brown and a black crayon for me.]

Inv. If you had to tell somebody what color you are, what word would you use?

J [She picks the brown crayon.]

Inv. What do you think it means when somebody says you're black?

J Somebody could say I'm black, but, um, I'm not. I'm brown.

Inv. Can you tell me what the word *race* means?

J Race? A race, um, a race where you could, um, if somebody runs far when you try to beat them.

Inv. Last time you drew for me, you drew a picture of yourself and you told me you had brown skin. Why was it important for you to tell me that?

J 'Cause that's the color skin I got. My mommy told me if I cry, my tears would melt all my skin and I would be a skeleton. [She wants to draw another picture. This time, it is one of polka dots.]

Inv. What color are your mommy and daddy?

J Brown, but my brother and Daddy are darker brown.

Inv. Are there different kinds of brown people?

J Some are darker, and some are lighter. Me and Mommy are light, and Daddy and my brother are darker.

Inv. Why do you think you and your brother are different shades of brown?

J I don't know.

(I decided this question was too difficult to comprehend, so I moved on to the subject of procreation.)

Inv. Do you think your mommy could have a white baby?

J [She shakes her head no.] She could have a boy baby or a girl baby.

Inv. Do you think mommies and daddies should be the same color?

J Yes.

Inv. Would it be all right if they were different colors?

J No, 'cause if they're different colors, then everybody would laugh at you. [She becomes involved again in making polka dots.]

(She asks to leave, and M, a European American boy, takes her place beside me.)

Inv. Are there different kinds of people?

M No, yes.

Inv. What kinds are there?

M Black people, white, and brown.

Inv. What is the difference between black people and white people?

M One's brown, and one's white. That's me. [He is pointing to his drawing.]

Inv. If I asked you what the word *black* means to you, what would you say?

M Green, white, black. [He is naming the crayon colors in his box.]

Inv. If someone said the word *black* to you, what do you think they mean?

M B-l-a-c-k. [He is spelling the word, using the crayon box as a guideline.]

Inv. If you had your choice, would you rather be white or black?

M Stay white.

Inv. Why?

M 'Cause I'm white.

Inv. If you were to describe yourself, how would you do that? Please tell me about M.

M Um, I have a sister, and her name is J, like J in our class. [He is pointing to his classmate outside.] And I have a boat, my dad's boat, not mine. My sister has a boat, a little boat.

Inv. If you had a girlfriend, would she have to be the same color as you?

M No. It would be okay if she was different.

Inv. Would you ever choose a black girlfriend?

M Yeah.

Inv. How would you feel about her?

M Good. I forgot to make my hair.

Inv. What do you think the word *race* means?

M Like having a race and see who wins.

Inv. You said girlfriends and boyfriends could be different colors. What about mommies and daddies?

M They could be different.

(F comes inside from outdoor play and sits down with the investigator and M.)

Inv. [to F] Do you think your mommy could have a black baby?

F Yeah, I was at my baby-sitter's house and there was this mommy that's white and the baby's brown. They can be different colors.

Inv. Do you think I could have a brown or black baby?

F Yes. You can have a white baby or a black baby or a brown baby. They don't have to be the same color as the mommy.

(End of playtime.)

References

Aboud, F. (1977). Interest in ethnic information: A cross-cultural developmental study. *Canadian Journal of Behavioral Science, 9,* 134-146.

Aboud, F. (1987). The development of ethnic self-identification and attitudes. In J. Phinney & M. Rotheram (Eds.), *Children's ethnic socialization: Pluralism and development* (pp. 32-55). Newbury Park, CA: Sage.

Aboud, F. (1988). *Children and prejudice.* New York: Basil Blackwell.

Aboud, F., & Skerry, S. (1984). The development of ethnic attitudes: A critical review. *Journal of Cross-Cultural Psychology, 15,* 3-34.

Adair, A., & Savage, J. (1973). Sex and race as determinants of preferences, attitudes, and self-identity among black preschool children: A developmental study. *Proceedings of the 81st Annual Convention of the American Psychological Association* (Vol. 8, pp. 651-652). Montreal, Canada.

Agar, M. (1980). *The professional stranger.* New York: Academic Press.

Altman, H. (1981). Individualized instruction and "back to basics": Reconciling paradoxes. *Journal of College Science Teaching, 11,* 20-24.

Amsterdam, B. (1972). Mirror self-image reactions before age two. *Developmental Psychology, 5,* 297-305.

Anderson, D., & Collins, P. (1988). *The impact on children's education: Television's influence on cognitive development.* Washington, DC: U.S. Department of Education, Office of Educational Research and Improvement.

Anderson, D., & Smith, R. (1984). Young children's TV viewing: The problem of cognitive continuity. In F. Morrison, C. Lord, & D. Keating (Eds.), *Applied developmental psychology* (Vol. 1, pp. 116-163). New York: Academic Press.

Anderson, E. (1975). Learning that boundaries are vague. *Journal of Child Language, 2,* 79-103.

Argyle, M., & Henderson, M. (1984). The rules of friendship. *Journal of Personal and Social Relationships, 1,* 211-237.

Argyle, M., Henderson, M., & Furnham, A. (1985). The rules of social relationships. *British Journal of Social Psychology, 24,* 125-139.

Arkin, R., & Burger, J. (1980). Effects of unit relation tendencies on interpersonal attraction. *Social Psychology Quarterly, 43,* 380-391.

Aronson, E. (1986). Applications of social psychology. *Communicating with the public.* Symposium conducted at the meeting of the Society of Experimental Social Psychology, Tempe, AZ.

Asher, S., & Allen, V. (1969). Racial preference and social comparison processes. *Journal of Social Issues, 25,* 157-166.

Asher, S., Singleton, L., & Taylor, A. (1982). *Acceptance vs. friendship: A longitudinal study of racial integration.* Paper presented at the meeting of the American Educational Research Association, New York.

Bandura, A. (1977). *Social learning theory.* Englewood Cliffs, NJ: Prentice Hall.

Bandura, A. (1986). *Social foundations of thought and action: A social cognitive theory.* Englewood Cliffs, NJ: Prentice Hall.

Barnett, D. (1982). The effects of open-space versus traditional self-contained classrooms on the auditory selective attending skills of elementary school children. *Language, Speech and Hearing Services in the Schools, 13,* 138-143.

Baron, R., & Byrne, D. (1991). *Social psychology: Understanding human interaction.* Boston: Allyn & Bacon.

Barth, F. (Ed.). (1969). *Ethnic groups and boundaries: The social organization of cultural difference.* Boston: Little, Brown.

Barth, F. (1992, November). *Ethnic groups and boundaries: Twenty years later.* Distinguished Lecture delivered at the 90th Annual Meeting of the American Anthropological Association, Chicago.

Berenthal, B., & Fisher, K. (1978). Development of self recognition in the infant. *Developmental Psychology, 14,* 44-50.

Berentzen, S. (1989). *Ethnographic approaches to children's worlds and peer cultures.* Trondheim, Norway: Norwegian Center for Child Research.

Berlin, B., & Kay, P. (1991). *Basic color terms: Their universality and evolution* (2nd ed.). Berkeley: University of California Press.

Berndt, T., & Hoyle, S. (1985). Stability and change in childhood and adolescent friendships. *Developmental Psychology, 21,* 1007-1015.

Best, R. (1983). *We've all got scars.* Bloomington: Indiana University Press.

Biafora, F., Taylor, D., Warheit, G., Zimmerman, R., & Vega, W. (1993). Cultural mistrust and racial awareness among ethnically diverse black adolescent boys. *Journal of Black Psychology, 19,* 266-282.

Bierman, K., & Schwartz, L. (1986). Clinical child interviews: Approaches and developmental considerations. *Child and Adolescent Psychotherapy, 3,* 267-278.

Billings, J. (1992). Racism in the '90s: Is it hip to hate? *Education Digest, 58,* 35-40.

Blanchard, K. (1986). Play as adaptation: The work/play dichotomy revisited. In B. Mergen (Ed.), *Cultural dimensions of play, games, and sport* (TASSP Vol. 10, pp. 79-87). Champaign, IL: Human Kinetics.

Bornstein, R. (1989). Overview and meta-analysis of research. *Psychological Reports, 106,* 265-289.

Bowman, P., & Howard, C. (1985). Race related socialization, motivation, and academic achievement: A study of black youth in three-generational families. *Journal of the American Academy of Child Psychiatry, 24,* 134-141.

Branch, C., & Newcombe, N. (1986). Racial attitude development among young black children as a function of parental attitudes: A longitudinal and cross-sectional study. *Child Development, 57,* 712-721.

Bredekamp, S. (1987). *Developmentally appropriate practice in early childhood programs serving children from birth through age 8.* Washington, DC: NAEYC.

Brehm, S. (1985). *Intimate relationships.* New York: Random House.

Breslin, F. (1981). "Back to basics": Education's brave new world. *New Jersey Education Association Review, 54,* 12-13.

Bretherton, I. (1984). *Symbolic play.* New York: Academic Press.

Brome, D. (1989). A developmental analysis of black children's others' concept. *Journal of Black Psychology, 15,* 149-162.

Bruner, J., Goodnow, J., & Austin, G. (1956). *A study of thinking.* New York: John Wiley.

Bruner, J., Goodnow, J., & Austin, G. (1972). Categories and cognition. In J. Spradley (Ed.), *Culture and cognition: Rules, maps, and plans* (pp. 168-190). New York: Holt, Rinehart & Winston.

Buettner-Janusch, J. (1966). *Origins of man.* New York: John Wiley.

Bullock, M., & Lutkenhaus, P. (1990). Who am I? Self-understanding in toddlers. *Merrill-Palmer Quarterly, 36,* 217-238.

Bunton, P., & Weissbach, T. (1974). Attitudes toward blackness of black preschool children attending community-controlled or public schools. *Journal of Social Psychology, 92,* 53-59.

Burling, R. (1969). Linguistics and ethnographic description. *American Anthropologist, 71,* 817-827.

Burns, R. (1979). *The self-concept: Theory, measurement, development, and behavior.* New York: Longman.

Butler, R. (1989). Mastery versus ability appraisal: A developmental study of children's observations of peers' work. *Child Development, 60,* 1350-1361.

Byrne, D. (1965). Parental antecedents of authoritarianism. *Journal of Personality and Social Psychology, 1,* 369-373.

Caldwell, B. (1989). All-day kindergarten: Assumptions, precautions, and overgeneralizations. *Early Childhood Research Quarterly, 4,* 261-267.

Calvert, S., & Gersh, T. (1987). The selective use of sound effects and visual inserts for children's television story comprehension. *Journal of Applied Developmental Psychology, 8,* 363-374.

Carey, J. (1989). *Communication as culture: Essays on media and society.* Boston: Little, Brown.

Caspi, A., & Herbener, E. (1990). Continuity and change: Assortative marriage and the consistency of personality in adulthood. *Journal of Personality and Social Psychology, 58,* 250-258.

Chagnon, N. (1977). *Yanomamo: The fierce people* (2nd ed.). New York: Holt, Rinehart & Winston.

Chick, G. (1989). On the categorization of games. *Play & Culture, 2,* 283-291.

Clark, A., Hocevar, D., & Dembo, M. (1980). The role of cognitive development in children's preferences for skin color. *Developmental Psychology, 16,* 332-339.

Clark, K. (1966). *Prejudice and your child* (2nd ed.). Boston: Beacon.

Clark, K., & Clark, M. (1947). Racial identification and preference in Negro children. In T. Newcomb & E. Hartley (Eds.), *Readings in social psychology* (pp. 169-178). New York: Holt.

Coles, R. (1964). *Children of crisis: A study of courage and fear.* Boston: Little, Brown.

Comstock, G., & Paik, H. (1991). *Television and the American child.* New York: Academic Press.

Cook, S. (1984). Cooperative interaction in multiethnic contexts. In N. Miller & M. Brewer (Eds.), *Groups in contact* (pp. 156-186). New York: Academic Press.

Cook, S. (1985). *Helping and being helped in cooperating interracial groups: Effects on respect and liking for group members.* Paper presented at the meeting of the Society of Experimental Social Psychology, Evanston, IL.

Corenblum, B., & Annis, R. (1987). Racial identity and preference in Native and white Canadian children. *Canadian Journal of Behavioral Science, 19,* 254-265.

Corenblum, B., & Wilson, A. (1982). Ethnic preference and identification among Canadian Indian and white children: Replication and extension. *Canadian Journal of Behavioral Science, 14,* 50-59.

Corsaro, W. (1985). *Friendship and peer culture in the early years.* Norwood, NJ: Ablex.

Corsaro, W., & Eder, D. (1990). Children's peer cultures. *Annual Review of Sociology, 16,* 197-220.

Cross, W. (1985). Black identity: Rediscovering the distinction between personal identity and reference group orientation. In M. Spencer, G. Brookins, & W. Allen (Eds.), *Beginnings: The social and affective development of black children* (pp. 155-171). Hillsdale, NJ: Lawrence Erlbaum.

Cunningham, B., & Wiegel, J. (1992). Preschool work and play activities: Child and teacher perspectives. *Play & Culture, 5,* 92-99.

Damon, W., & Hart, D. (1982). The development of self-understanding from infancy through adolescence. *Child Development, 53,* 841-864.

Damon, W., & Hart, D. (1988). *Self-understanding in childhood and adolescence.* New York: Cambridge University Press.

Deegan, J. (1991, April). *An ethnography of children's friendships in a fifth-grade culturally diverse class.* Paper presented at the Annual Meeting of the American Educational Research Association, Chicago.

Deegan, J. (1993). Children's friendships in culturally diverse classrooms. *Journal of Research in Childhood Education, 7,* 91.

Devine, P. (1989). Stereotypes and prejudice: Their automatic and controlled components. *Journal of Personality and Social Psychology, 56,* 5-18.

Dion, K. (1980). Physical attractiveness, sex roles, and heterosexual attraction. In M. Cook (Ed.), *The bases of human sexual attraction* (pp. 3-22). New York: Academic Press.

Dion, K. (1986). Stereotyping based on physical attractiveness: Issues and conceptual perspectives. In C. Herman, M. Zanna, & E. Higgins (Eds.), *Physical appearance, stigma, and social behavior: The Ontario Symposium on Personality and Social Psychology* (Vol. 3, pp. 7-21). Hillsdale, NJ: Lawrence Erlbaum.

Dougherty, J. (1985). *Directions in cognitive anthropology.* Chicago: University of Illinois Press.

Draper, P. (1985). Two views of sex differences in socialization. In R. Hall, P. Draper, M. Hamilton, D. McGuinness, C. Otten, & E. Roth (Eds.), *Male-female differences: A bio-cultural perspective* (pp. 5-25). New York: Praeger.

Drewry, D., & Clark, M. (1984, April). *Similarity effects and age differences in children's friendships.* Paper presented at the 68th Annual Meeting of the American Educational Research Association, New Orleans.

Eder, D., & Hallinan, M. (1978). Sex differences in children's friendships. *American Sociological Review, 43,* 237-250.

Eder, R. (1989). The emerging personologist: The structure and content of 3 ½-, 5 ½-, and 7 ½-year-olds' concepts of themselves and other persons. *Child Development, 60,* 1218-1228.

Eder, R. (1990). Uncovering young children's psychological selves: Individual and developmental differences. *Child Development, 61,* 849-863.

Eder, R., Gerlack, S., & Perlmutter, M. (1987). In search of children's selves: Development of the specific and general components of the self-concept. *Child Development, 61,* 849-863.

Elkind, D. (1981). *The hurried child.* Reading, MA: Addison-Wesley.

Epstein, J., & Karweit, N. (1983). *Friends in school.* New York: Academic Press.

Erikson, E. (1963). *Childhood and society* (2nd ed.). New York: Norton.

Estes, D., Wellman, H., & Wooley, J. (1989). Children's understanding of mental phenomena. In H. Reese (Ed.), *Advances in child development and behavior* (Vol. 22, pp. 41-87). New York: Academic Press.

Everhart, R. (1983). *Reading, writing, and resistance.* Boston: Routledge & Kegan Paul.

Falbo, T. (1980). A social psychological model of human sexuality. In J. Parsons (Ed.), *The psychobiology of sex differences and sex roles* (pp. 131-142). New York: McGraw-Hill.

Feingold, A. (1988). Matching for attractiveness in romantic partner and same-sex friends: A meta-analysis and theoretical critique. *Psychological Bulletin, 104,* 226-235.

Fine, G. (1980). Cracking diamonds: Observer role in Little League baseball settings and the acquisition of social competence. In W. Shaffir, A. Turowetz, & R. Stebbins (Eds.), *The social experience of fieldwork* (pp. 117-181). New York: St. Martin's.

Fine, G. (1987). *With the boys.* Chicago: University of Chicago Press.

Fine, G., & Sandstrom, K. (1988). *Knowing children: Participant observation with minors.* Newbury Park, CA: Sage.

Freeman, N. (1987). Current problems in the development of representational picture production. *Archives de Psychologie, 55,* 127-152.

Gardner, H. (1980). *Artful scribbles.* New York: Basic Books.

Geertz, C. (1973). *The interpretation of cultures.* New York: Basic Books.

Gerard, H. (1983). School desegregation: The social science role. *American Psychologist, 38,* 869-877.

Gerard, H., & Miller, N. (1975). *School desegregation.* New York: Plenum.

Gesell, A., & Ilg, F. (1946). *The child from five to ten.* New York: Harper & Row.

Glassner, B. (1976). Kid society. *Urban Education, 11,* 5-22.

Goleman, D. (1989, September 5). Psychologists find ways to break racism's hold. *New York Times,* pp. C1, C8.

Goode, D. (1986). Kids, culture, and innocents. *Human Studies, 9,* 83-106.

Goodenough, W. (1956). Residence rules. *Southwestern Journal of Anthropology, 12,* 22-37.

Goodenough, W. (1957). Cultural anthropology and linguistics. In P. Garvin (Ed.), *Report of the Seventh Annual Round Table Meeting on Linguistics and Language Study.* Washington, DC: Georgetown University.

Goodman, M. (1952). *Race awareness in young children.* New York: Collier.

Goodnow, J. (1977). *Children's drawing.* Cambridge, MA: Harvard University Press.

Gottman, J. (1983). How children become friends. *Monographs of the Society for Research in Child Development, 48*(3, Serial No. 201).

Granucci, P. (1990). Kindergarten teachers: Working through our identity crisis. *Young Children, 45,* 6-11.

Greenberg, B. (1986). Minorities and the mass media. In J. Bryant & D. Zillmann (Eds.), *Perspectives on media effects* (pp. 165-188). Hillsdale, NJ: Lawrence Erlbaum.

Gump, P. (1978). School environments. In I. Altman & J. Wohlwill (Eds.), *Children and the environment* (pp. 131-174). New York: Plenum.

Gurkin, S. (1968). *The effects of the race of the interviewer in a study of race awareness in Caucasian children.* Senior thesis, Randolph-Macon Woman's College, Lynchburg, VA.

Hall, E. (1959). *The silent language.* Garden City, NY: Doubleday.

Hallinan, M., & Smith, S. (1985). The effects of classroom racial composition on students' interracial friendliness. *Social Psychology Quarterly, 48,* 3-16.

Hallinan, M., & Teixeira, R. (1987). Students' interracial friendships: Individual characteristics, structural effects, and racial differences. *American Journal of Education, 95,* 563-583.

Hallinan, M., & Williams, R. (1987). The stability of students' interracial friendships. *American Sociological Review, 52,* 653-664.

Harrison, J. (1981). The impact of open and traditional classrooms on achievement and creativity: The Israeli case. *Elementary School Journal, 82,* 27-35.

Harter, S. (1983). Developmental perspectives on the self-system. In P. Mussen & E. Hetherington (Eds.), *Handbook of child psychology: Vol. 4. Socialization, personality, and social development* (pp. 275-385). New York: John Wiley.

Harter, S. (1988). Developmental processes in the construction of self. In T. Yawkey & J. Johnson (Eds.), *Integrative processes and socialization* (pp. 43-70). Hillsdale, NJ: Lawrence Erlbaum.

Hatch, J., & Freeman, E. (1988). Kindergarten philosophies and practices: Perspectives of teachers, principals, and supervisors. *Early Childhood Research Quarterly, 3,* 151-166.

Hawley, W. (1988). Why is it hard to believe in desegregation? *Equity and Choice, 4,* 11-14.

Hays, R. (1985). A longitudinal study of friendship development. *Journal of Personality and Social Psychology, 48,* 909-924.

Hearold, S. (1986). A synthesis of 1043 effects of television on social behavior. In G. Comstock (Ed.), *Public communication and behavior* (Vol. 1, pp. 65-133). New York: Academic Press.

Hewitt, R. (1986). *White talk, black talk: Interracial friendship and communication amongst adolescents.* New York: Cambridge University Press.

Hollifield, J., & Slavin, R. (1983). Disseminating student team learning through federally funded programs: Appropriate technology, appropriate channels. *Knowledge, 4,* 576-589.

Holmes, R. (1990). Social interaction in kindergarten: The rules of friendship. *Education, 26,* 158-162.

Holmes, R. (1991a). Categories of play: A kindergartner's analysis. *Play & Culture, 4,* 43-50.

Holmes, R. (1991b). A lesson learned: Teacher's aide or child's aide. *Intervention in School and Clinic, 26*(3), 159-161.

Holmes, R. (1992a). Children's artwork and nonverbal communication. *Child Study Journal, 22,* 157-166.

Holmes, R. (1992b). Play during snacktime. *Play & Culture, 5,* 295-304.

Hunsberger, B. (1978). Racial awareness and preference of white and Indian Canadian children. *Canadian Journal of Behavioral Science, 10,* 176-179.

Ignico, A. (1990). The influence of gender-role perception on activity preferences of children. *Play & Culture, 3,* 302-310.

Interracial dating: Yes or no? (1993). *The Black Collegian, 23,* 31-35.

Jacobsen, D. (1975). Fair weather friend: Label and context in middle-class friendships. *Journal of Anthropological Research, 31,* 225-234.

Johnson, C., & Wellman, H. (1982). Children's developing conceptions of the mind and brain. *Child Development, 53,* 222-234.

Johnson, D., & Johnson, R. (1981). Effects of cooperative and individualistic learning experiences on inter-ethnic interaction. *Journal of Educational Psychology, 73,* 444-449.

Johnson, J. (1975). *Doing field research.* New York: Free Press.

Johnston, J. (1982). *Positive images: Breaking stereotypes with children's television.* Beverly Hills, CA: Sage.

Jones, G. (1983). Identifying basic categories. *Psychological Bulletin, 1-94,* 423-428.

Jones, M. (1968). *The effects of the race of the interviewer in a study of race awareness in Negro children.* Senior thesis, Randolph-Macon Woman's College, Lynchburg, VA.

Judd, C., & Park, B. (1988). Out-group homogeneity: Judgments of variability at the individual and group levels. *Journal of Personality and Social Psychology, 54,* 778-788.

Kagan, J. (1984). *The nature of the child.* New York: Basic Books.

Kamii, C. (1985). Leading primary education toward excellence. *Young Children, 40,* 3-9.

Katz, P., & Taylor, D. (1988). *Eliminating racism.* New York: Plenum.

Keesing, R. (1972). Simple models of complexity: The lure of kinship. In P. Reining (Ed.), *Kinship studies in the Morgan Centennial Year* (pp. 17-32). Washington, DC: Anthropological Society of Washington.

Kellogg, R. (1969). *The psychology of children's drawings.* New York: Random House.

Kelly-Byrne, D. (1989). *A child's play life: An ethnographic study.* New York: Teachers College Press.

Kempton, W. (1978). Category grading and taxonomic relations: A mug is a sort of a cup. *American Ethnologist, 5,* 44-65.

King, N. (1982). Children's conceptions of work and play. *Social Education, 46,* 110-113.

King, N. (1987). Elementary school play: Theory and research. In J. Block & N. King (Eds.), *School play: A source book* (Vol. 10, pp. 143-165). New York: Garland.

Kohlberg, L. (1966). A cognitive developmental analysis of children's sex role concepts and attitudes. In E. Maccoby (Ed.), *The development of sex differences* (pp. 81-173). Stanford, CA: Stanford University Press.

Kohlberg, L. (1976). Moral stages and moralization: The cognitive-developmental approach. In T. Lickona (Ed.), *Moral development and behavior* (pp. 31-53). New York: Holt, Rinehart & Winston.

Konner, M. (1991). *Childhood.* Boston: Little, Brown.

Kottak, C. (1990). *Prime-time society: An anthropological analysis of television and culture.* Belmont, CA: Wadsworth.

Kurth, S. (1970). Friendship and friendly relations. In G. McCall, M. McCall, N. Denzin, G. Suttles, & S. Kurth (Eds.), *Social relationships* (pp. 136-170). Hawthorne, NY: Aldine.

LaGaipa, J. (1977). Interpersonal attraction and social exchange. In S. Duck (Ed.), *Theory and practice in interpersonal attraction* (pp. 129-164). New York: Academic Press.

Langer, D. (1985). Children's legal rights as research subjects. *Journal of the American Academy of Child Psychiatry, 24,* 653-662.

Leary, M., Rogers, P., Canfield, R., & Coe, C. (1986). Boredom in interpersonal encounters: Antecedents and social implications. *Journal of Personality and Social Psychology, 51,* 968-975.

Levine, R., & White, M. (1986). *Human conditions: The cultural basis for educational development.* New York: Routledge & Kegan Paul.

Lewis, M., & Brooks-Gunn, J. (1972, April). *Self, other, and fear: The reaction of infants to people.* Paper presented at the meetings of the Eastern Psychological Association, Boston.

Lewis, M., & Brooks-Gunn, J. (1979). *Social cognition and the acquisition of self.* New York: Plenum.

Llewellyn, M. (1980). Studying girls at school: The implications of confusion. In R. Deem (Ed.), *Schooling for women's work* (pp. 42-51). London: Routledge & Kegan Paul.

Lodziak, C. (1986). *The power of television.* New York: Holt, Rinehart & Winston.

Loftus, E. (1975). Leading questions and the eyewitness report. *Cognitive Psychology, 7,* 560-572.

Maccoby, E. (1990). Gender and relationships: A developmental account. *American Psychologist, 45,* 513-520.

Maccoby, E., & Jacklin, C. (1987). Gender segregation in childhood. In H. Reese (Ed.), *Advances in child development* (Vol. 20, pp. 239-287). New York: Academic Press.

Magaro, P., & Ashbrook, R. (1985). The personality of societal groups. *Journal of Personality and Social Psychology, 48,* 1479-1489.

Mandell, N. (1988). The least-adult role in studying children. *Journal of Contemporary Ethnography, 16,* 433-467.

Mandler, J. (1990). A new perspective on cognitive development in infancy. *American Scientist, 78,* 236-243.

Maybury-Lewis, D., & Almagor, U. (1989). *The attraction of opposites: Thought and society in the dualistic mode.* Ann Arbor: University of Michigan Press.

McCandless, B., & Evans, E. (1973). *Children and youth.* Hillsdale, IL: Dryden.

McTeer, H., & Beaver, S. (1981, April-June). A comparison of open space and closed space classrooms in social studies instruction. *Resources in Education, 16,* 180.

Medin, D., & Smith, E. (1984). Concepts and concept formation. *Annual Review of Psychology, 35,* 113-138.

Mervis, C. (1987). Child basic object categories and early lexical development. In U. Neisser (Ed.), *Concepts and conceptual development: Ecological and intellectual factors in categorization* (pp. 201-233). Cambridge, England: Cambridge University Press.

Miller, A. (1982). *In the eye of the beholder: Contemporary issues in stereotyping.* New York: Praeger.

Minuchin, P., & Shapiro, E. (1983). The school as a context for social development. In E. M. Hetherington (Ed.), *Handbook of child psychology: Vol. 4. Socialization, personality, and social development* (pp. 197-274). New York: John Wiley.

Moore, C. (1976). The racial preference and attitude of preschool black children. *Journal of Genetic Psychology, 129,* 37-44.

Morland, J. (1966). A comparison of race awareness in Northern and Southern children. *American Journal of Orthopsychiatry, 36,* 22-31.

Morland, J., & Hwang, C. (1981). Racial/ethnic identity of preschool children. *Journal of Cross-Cultural Psychology, 12,* 409-424.

Moyer, J., Egertson, H., & Isenberg, J. (1987). The child-centered kindergarten. *Childhood Education, 63,* 235-242.

Murphy, D. (1985). Brief communication. *Human Organization, 44,* 132-137.

Murstein, B. (1986). *Paths to marriage.* Newbury Park, CA: Sage.

Murstein, B., Merighi, J., & Malloy, T. (1989). Physical attractiveness and exchange theory in interracial dating. *Journal of Social Psychology, 129,* 325-335.

Nall, S. (1982). Bridging the gap: Preschool to kindergarten. *Childhood Education, 59,* 107-110.

National Association for the Education of Young Children (NAEYC). (1988). NAEYC position statement on developmentally appropriate practices in the primary grades, serving 5- through 8-year-olds. *Young Children, 43,* 64-83.

Needham, R. (1973). *Right and left: Essays on dual symbolic classification.* Chicago: University of Chicago Press.

Needham, R. (1979). *Symbolic classification.* Santa Monica, CA: Goodyear.

Needham, R. (1980). *Reconnaissances.* Toronto: University of Toronto Press.

Neisser, U. (1988). Five kinds of self knowledge. *Philosophical Psychology, 1,* 35-59.

Newcomb, T. (1961). *The acquaintance process.* New York: Holt, Rinehart & Winston.

Newcomb, T. (1981). Heiderian balance as a group phenomenon. *Journal of Personality and Social Psychology, 40,* 862-867.

O'Bryan-Garland, S., & Parkay, F. (1985). Back to basics: Reflections on the past and a glimpse into the future. *NASSP Bulletin, 69,* 28-33.

Olsen, D., & Zigler, E. (1989). An assessment of the all-day kindergarten movement. *Early Childhood Research Quarterly, 4,* 167-187.

Parker, W. (1984). Interviewing children: Problems and promise. *Journal of Negro Education, 53,* 18-28.

Paset, P., & Taylor, R. (1991). Black and white women's attitudes toward interracial marriage. *Psychological Reports, 69,* 753-756.

Peck, J., McCaig, G., & Sapp, M. (1988). *Kindergarten policies: What is best for children?* Washington, DC: NAEYC.

Pettigrew, T. (1986). The intergroup contact hypothesis reconsidered. In M. Hewston & R. Brown (Eds.), *Contact and conflict in intergroup encounter* (pp. 169-195). New York: Basil Blackwell.

Phinney, J. (1989). Stages of ethnic identity development in minority group adolescents. *Journal of Early Adolescence, 9,* 34-49.

Phinney, J., & Rotheram, M. (1987). *Children's ethnic socialization.* Newbury Park, CA: Sage.

Piaget, J. (1963). *The origins of intelligence in children* (2nd ed.). New York: Norton.

Piaget, J. (1965). *The child's conception of the world.* Paterson, NJ: Littlefield, Adams.

Priest, R., & Sawyer, J. (1967). Proximity and peership: Bases of balance in interpersonal attraction. *American Journal of Sociology, 72,* 633-649.

Quattrone, G. (1986). On the perception of a group's variability. In S. Worchel & W. Austin (Eds.), *Psychology of intergroup relations* (pp. 25-48). Chicago: Nelson-Hall.

Quattrone, G., & Jones, E. (1980). The perception of variability within ingroups and outgroups: Implications for the law of small numbers. *Journal of Personality and Social Psychology, 38,* 141-152.

Raman, A. (1984). Psychological aspects of racism in the international perspective. *International Journal of Social Psychiatry, 30,* 148-152.

Ramsey, P. (1987). Young children's thinking about ethnic differences. In J. Phinney & M. Rotheram (Eds.), *Children's ethnic socialization* (pp. 56-72). Newbury Park, CA: Sage.

Rizzo, T. (1989). *Friendship development among children at school.* Norwood, NJ: Ablex.

Roosens, E. (1989). *Creating ethnicity: The process of ethnogenesis.* Newbury Park, CA: Sage.

Rosch, E. (1973). On the internal structure of perceptual and semantic categories. In T. Moore (Ed.), *Cognitive development and the acquisition of language* (pp. 111-114). New York: Academic Press.

Rosch, E., & Lloyd, B. (1978). *Cognition and categorization.* Hillsdale, NJ: LEA.

Rosch, E., Mervis, C., Gray, W., Johnson, D., & Boyes-Braem, P. (1976). Basic objects in natural categories. *Cognitive Psychology, 8,* 382-439.

Rosenberg, M. (1979). *Conceiving the self.* New York: Basic Books.

Royce, A. (1982). *Ethnic identity: Strategies of diversity.* Bloomington: Indiana University Press.

Rubin, Z. (1980). *Children's friendships.* Cambridge, MA: Harvard University Press.

Ruble, D. (1987). The acquisition of self-knowledge: A self-socialization process. In N. Eisenberg (Ed.), *Contemporary topics in developmental psychology* (pp. 243-270). New York: John Wiley.

Russell, K., & Wilson, M. (1992). *The color complex.* New York: Harcourt Brace Jovanovich.

Rutter, M., Maugham, B., Mortimore, P., & Ouston, J. (1979). *Fifteen thousand hours: Secondary school and their effect on children.* London: Open Books.

Saegert, S., Swap, W., & Zajonc, R. (1973). Exposure, context, and interpersonal attraction. *Journal of Personality and Social Psychology, 25,* 234-242.

Sagar, H., Schofield, J., & Snyder, H. (1983). Race and gender barriers: Preadolescent peer behavior in academic classrooms. *Child Development, 54,* 1032-1040.

Schofield, J. (1979). The impact of positively structured contact on intergroup behavior: Does it last under adverse conditions? *Social Psychology Quarterly, 42,* 280-284.

Schofield, J. (1984). Complementary and conflicting identities. In S. Asher & J. Gottman (Eds.), *The development of children's friendships* (pp. 53-90). Cambridge, England: Cambridge University Press.

Schofield, J. (1986). Black-white contact in desegregated schools. In M. Hewstone & R. Brown (Eds.), *Contact and conflict in intergroup encounters* (pp. 79-92). New York: Basil Blackwell.

Schofield, J. (1989). *Black and white in school: Trust, tension, or tolerance?* New York: Teachers College Press.

Schofield, J. (1993). Promoting positive peer relations in desegregated schools. *Educational Policy, 7,* 297-317.

Schofield, J., & Francis, W. (1982). An observational study of peer interaction in racially mixed "accelerated" classrooms. *Journal of Educational Psychology, 74,* 722-732.

Schwartzman, H. (1978). *Transformations.* New York: Plenum.

Selman, R. (1980). *The growth of interpersonal understanding: Developmental and clinical analyses.* New York: Academic Press.

Selman, R. (1990). *Making a friend in youth: Developmental theory and pair therapy.* Chicago: University of Chicago Press.

Semaj, L. (1980). The development of racial evaluation and preference: A cognitive approach. *Journal of Black Psychology, 6,* 59-79.

Semaj, L. (1985). Afrikanity, cognition, and extended self-identity. In M. Spencer, G. Brookins, & W. Allen (Eds.), *Beginnings: The social and affective development of black children* (pp. 173-184). Hillsdale, NJ: Lawrence Erlbaum.

Sherif, M., Harvey, O., White, B., Hood, W., & Sherif, R. (1961). *Intergroup conflict and cooperation: The Robbers Cave experiment.* Norman, OK: Institute of Group Relations.

Sigelman, L., & Welch, S. (1993). The contact hypothesis revisited: Black-white interaction and positive racial attitudes. *Social Forces, 71,* 781-796.

Silberman, C. (1970). *Crisis in the classroom: The remaking of American education.* New York: Random House.

Simon, B., & Brown, R. (1987). Perceived intragroup homogeneity in minority majority contexts. *Journal of Personality and Social Psychology, 53,* 703-711.

Singh, B. (1991). Teaching methods for reducing prejudice and enhancing academic achievement for all children. *Educational Studies, 17,* 157-191.

Singleton, L., & Asher, S. (1979). Racial integration and children's peer preferences: An investigation of developmental and cohort differences. *Child Development, 50,* 936-941.

Slaughter, D., & McWorter, G. (1985). Social origins and early features of the scientific study of black American families and children. In M. Spencer, G. Brookins, & W. Allen (Eds.), *Beginnings: The social and affective development of black children* (pp. 5-18). Hillsdale, NJ: Lawrence Erlbaum.

Slavin, R. (1983). *Cooperative learning.* New York: Longman.

Slavin, R. (1986). Cooperative learning: Engineering social psychology in the classroom. In R. Feldman (Ed.), *The social psychology of education* (pp. 153-171). New York: Cambridge University Press.

Slavin, R. (1990). *Cooperative learning: Theory, research, and practice.* Englewood Cliffs, NJ: Prentice Hall.

Smith, D. (1987). *California kindergarten practices 1986.* Paper presented at the Annual Conference of the National Association for the Education of Young Children, Washington, DC.

Speier, M. (1976). The adult ideological viewpoint in studies of childhood. In A. Skolnick (Ed.), *Rethinking childhood* (pp. 168-186). Boston: Little, Brown.

Spencer, M. (1982). Personal and group identity of black children: An alternative synthesis. *Genetic Psychology Monographs, 103,* 59-84.

Spencer, M. (1983). Children's cultural values and parental child-rearing strategies. *Developmental Review, 3,* 351-379.

Spencer, M. (1984). Black children's race awareness, racial attitudes, and self-concept: An interpretation. *Journal of Child Psychology and Psychiatry, 25,* 433-441.

Spencer, M. (1985). Cultural cognition and social cognition as identity factors in black children's personal growth. In M. Spencer, G. Brookins, & W. Allen (Eds.), *Beginnings: The social and affective development of black children* (pp. 215-230). Hillsdale, NJ: Lawrence Erlbaum.

Spencer, M. (1988). Self-concept development. In D. Slaughter (Ed.), *Black children and poverty: A developmental perspective* (pp. 59-72). San Francisco: Jossey-Bass.

Spradley, J. (1972). *Culture and cognition: Rules, maps, and plans.* New York: Holt, Rinehart & Winston.

Spradley, J. (1980). *Participant observation.* New York: Holt, Rinehart & Winston.

Stephan, W. (1978). School desegregation: An examination of predictions made in Brown v. Board of Education. *Psychological Bulletin, 85,* 217-238.

Stephan, W., & Stephan, C. (1991). Intermarriage: Effects on personality, adjustment, and intergroup relations in two samples of students. *Journal of Marriage and the Family, 53,* 241-251.

St. John, N. (1975). *School desegregation: Outcomes for children.* New York: John Wiley.

St. John, N., & Lewis, R. (1975). Race and the social structure of the elementary classroom. *Sociology of Education, 48,* 346-368.

Stroman, C. (1986). Television viewing and self-concept among black children. *Journal of Broadcasting and Electronic Media, 30,* 87-93.

Sutton-Smith, B. (1979). The play of girls. In C. Kopp (Ed.), *Becoming female: Perspectives on development* (pp. 229-257). New York: Plenum.

Tajfel, H. (1981). *Human groups and social categories.* New York: Cambridge University Press.

Thomas, G., & Silk, A. (1990). *An introduction to the psychology of children's drawings.* New York: New York University Press.

Thompson, R. (1989). *Theories of ethnicity: A critical appraisal.* New York: Greenwood.

Turner, V., & Bruner, E. (1986). *The anthropology of experience.* Urbana: University of Illinois Press.

Tyler, S. (1969). *Cognitive anthropology.* New York: Holt, Rinehart & Winston.

U.S. Bureau of the Census. (1990). *Census of population and housing.* Washington, DC: Author.

Van Evra, J. (1990). *Television and child development.* Hillsdale, NJ: Lawrence Erlbaum.

Waksler, F. (1986). Studying children: Phenomenological insights. *Human Studies, 9,* 71-92.

Whitley, B., Schofield, J., & Snyder, H. (1984). Peer preferences in a desegregated school: A round robin analysis. *Journal of Personality and Social Psychology, 46,* 799-810.

Wieseman, R. (1986). Multicultural beginnings and early learning. *Journal of Instructional Psychology, 13,* 172-176.

Wilder, D. (1978). Perceiving persons as a group: Effects of attributions of causality and beliefs. *Social Psychology, 41,* 13-23.

Wilder, D. (1986). Social categorization: Implications for creation and reduction of intergroup bias. In L. Berkowitz (Ed.), *Advances in experimental social psychology* (Vol. 19, pp. 293-355). New York: Academic Press.

Williams, J., & Morland, J. (1976). *Race, color, and the young child.* Chapel Hill: University of North Carolina Press.

Worchel, S. (1986). The role of cooperation in reducing intergroup conflict. In S. Worchel & G. Austin (Eds.), *Psychology of intergroup relations* (pp. 288-304). Chicago: Nelson-Hall.

Worchel, S., Axsom, D., Ferris, F., Samaha, C., & Schweitzer, S. (1978). Factors determining the effect of intergroup cooperation on intergroup attraction. *Journal of Conflict Resolution, 22,* 429-439.

Zajonc, R. (1968). Attitudinal effects of mere exposure. *Journal of Personality and Social Psychology Monographs, 9*(2, Pt. 2).

Zajonc, R. (1980). Feeling and thinking: Preferences need no inferences. *American Psychologist, 35,* 151-175.

Author Index

Aboud, F., 1-3, 5, 19, 26, 30, 45, 59, 61, 63, 92, 98, 100-101, 103-104, 107-109
Adair, A., 34
Agar, M., 3, 9, 10, 12, 17, 63, 105
Allen, V., 1, 41, 104
Almagor, U., 34
Altman, H., 32
Amsterdam, B., 47
Anderson, D., 64
Anderson, E., 40, 88
Annis, R., 104
Argyle, M., 68, 74
Arkin, R., 31, 68
Aronson, E., 26, 107
Ashbrook, R., 26, 68
Asher, S., 1, 2, 41, 104
Austin, G., 39
Axsom, D., 61

Bandura, A., 47, 63, 110
Barnett, D., 32, 33
Baron, R., 70, 83
Barth, F., 4
Beaver, S., 32
Berenthal, B., 47
Berentzen, S., 3, 12, 105
Berlin, B., 40, 98, 99
Berndt, T., 31, 69, 75, 78
Best, R., 18
Biafora, F., 60
Bierman, K., 2, 13, 17
Billings, J., 86, 108
Black Collegian, The, 101
Blanchard, K., 33
Bornstein, R., 81
Bowman, P., 53
Boyes-Braem, P., 40
Branch, C., 2, 47, 53, 54, 85, 102
Bredekamp, S., 33
Brehm, S., 78
Breslin, F., 32
Bretherton, I., 30
Brome, D., 40, 58
Brooks-Gunn, J., 19, 47
Brown, R., 61
Bruner, E., 12, 13, 92, 110
Bruner, J., 39
Buettner-Janusch, J., 4
Bullock, M., 41, 48
Bunton, P., 101
Burger, J., 31, 68
Burling, R., 14
Burns, R., 41, 45, 47, 108
Butler, R., 26, 37, 41, 48, 63, 107
Byrne, D., 63, 70, 83

Caldwell, B., 27, 32
Calvert, S., 64
Canfield, R., 77
Carey, J., 64, 69
Caspi, A., 26, 68
Chagnon, N., 5, 15
Chick, G., 3

Clark, A., 18, 44
Clark, K., 2, 3, 19, 53
Clark, M., 2, 68, 78, 85
Coe, C., 77
Coles, R., 3, 13, 48, 98
Collins, P., 64
Comstock, G., 64, 65, 110
Cook, S., 19, 25, 26, 30, 77, 106, 107
Corenblum, B., 18, 104
Corsaro, W., 3, 9, 11-12, 17, 25, 38, 66-67, 72, 74-75
Cross, W., 51, 53, 59, 109
Cunningham, B., 33

Damon, W., 47, 51, 62
Deegan, J., 67-69, 75, 79, 80
Dembo, M., 18
Devine, P., 54, 65, 109
Dion, K., 70, 83, 84
Dougherty, J., 12
Draper, P., 35
Drewry, D., 68, 78, 85

Eder, D., 25, 78
Eder, R., 48, 66
Egertson, H., 33
Elkind, D., 32
Epstein, J., 30, 80
Erikson, E., 109
Estes, D., 48
Evans, E., 47
Everhart, R., 11

Falbo, T., 35
Feingold, A., 26, 68, 69, 107
Ferris, F., 61
Fine, G., 3, 8-12, 17, 18, 66, 105, 110
Fisher, K., 47
Francis, W., 2
Freeman, E., 33
Freeman, N., 4
Furnham, A., 74

Gardner, H., 3, 13
Geertz, C., 12
Gerard, H., 25, 26, 106
Gerlack, S., 48
Gersh, T., 64
Gesell, A., 38, 39, 66, 81, 88, 98
Glassner, B., 11
Goleman, D., 26, 30, 107
Goode, D., 12
Goodenough, W., 4, 12
Goodman, M., 1
Goodnow, J., 3, 13, 39
Gottman, J., 75
Granucci, P., 27, 32
Gray, W., 40
Greenberg, B., 64, 65, 85
Gump, P., 27, 80
Gurkin, S., 18

Hall, E., 81, 110
Hallinan, M., 25, 26, 31, 76, 78, 80, 106, 107, 109
Harrison, J., 32, 33
Hart, D., 47, 51, 62
Harter, S., 1, 26, 41, 45, 47, 48, 53, 63, 107-108
Harvey, O., 63
Hatch, J., 33
Hawley, W., 25, 106
Hays, R., 31, 68, 77, 80
Hearold, S., 64
Henderson, M., 68, 74
Herbener, E., 26, 68, 69
Hewitt, R., 61, 76, 78-80
Hocevar, D., 18
Hollifield, J., 26, 107
Holmes, R., 3-5, 11, 12, 14, 17, 18, 31, 40, 45, 74, 81
Hood, W., 63
Howard, C., 53
Hoyle, S., 31, 69, 75, 76, 78
Hunsberger, B., 104
Hwang, C., 1

Ignico, A., 93
Ilg, F., 38, 39, 66, 81, 88, 98
Isenberg, J., 33

Jacklin, C., 26, 36, 93
Jacobsen, D., 67, 74
Jones, E., 40, 61
Johnson, C., 48
Johnson, D., 19, 26, 40, 107

Johnson, J., 8, 12
Johnson, R., 19, 26, 107
Johnston, J., 65
Jones, G., 40
Jones, M., 18
Judd, C., 59, 61

Kagan, J., 35, 36, 39, 48, 81, 88, 93, 98
Kamii, C., 32
Karweit, N., 30, 80
Katz, P., 19, 25, 26, 106
Kay, P., 40, 98, 99
Keesing, R., 37, 46
Kellogg, R., 3, 13
Kelly-Byrne, D., 3, 11, 18
Kempton, W., 40, 88
King, N., 3, 33
Kohlberg, L., 35, 81, 104
Konner, M., 81
Kottak, C., 110
Kurth, S., 67

LaGaipa, J., 77
Langer, D., 9
Leary, M., 77, 80, 81
Levine, R., 51, 62
Lewis, M., 19, 47
Lewis, R., 2,
Llewellyn, M., 10
Lloyd, B., 5, 14, 40, 70, 99, 108
Lodziak, C., 64
Loftus, E., 2, 18
Lutkenhaus, P., 41, 48

Maccoby, E., 26, 36, 69, 93, 107
Magaro, P., 26, 68
Malloy, T., 84
Mandell, N., 3, 10
Mandler, J., 5, 40, 45
Maugham, B., 7
Maybury-Lewis, D., 34
McCaig, G., 32
McCandless, B., 47
McTeer, H., 32
McWorter, G., 53
Medin, D., 40
Merighi, J., 84
Mervis, C., 40, 45, 108, 109

Miller, A., 54, 64
Miller, N., 25
Minuchin, P., 26, 30, 33, 107
Moore, C., 18
Morland, J., 1, 4, 38, 41, 53, 63, 98, 108
Mortimore, P., 7
Moyer, J., 33
Murphy, D., 11, 17
Murstein, B., 84

Nall, S., 32
National Association for the Education of Young Children (NAEYC), 32
Needham, R., 34, 108
Neisser, U., 47
Newcomb, T., 31, 78, 80
Newcombe, N., 2, 47, 53, 54, 85, 102

O'Bryan-Garland, S., 32
Olsen, D., 31
Ouston, J., 7

Paik, H., 64, 65, 110
Park, B., 59, 61
Parkay, F., 32
Parker, W., 2, 13, 17
Paset, P., 85
Peck, J., 32
Perlmutter, M., 48
Pettigrew, T., 31, 109
Phinney, J., 4, 37, 47, 59, 102, 104
Piaget, J., 60, 62, 85, 88, 100, 102, 108-110
Priest, R., 31

Quattrone, G., 54, 61, 64, 109

Raman, A., 54, 63, 85, 92, 102, 104, 110
Ramsey, P., 26, 37, 41, 45, 63, 98, 104, 107-108
Rizzo, T., 8, 27, 30, 31, 66, 80
Rogers, P., 77
Roosens, E., 5
Rosch, E., 5, 14, 40, 46, 67, 70, 88, 99, 108
Rosenberg, M., 1
Rotheram, M., 4, 37, 102, 104
Royce, A., 5
Rubin, Z., 67, 75

Ruble, D., 41, 48
Russell, K., 44, 55
Rutter, M., 7

Saegert, S., 31
Sagar, H., 107
Samaha, C., 62
Sandstrom, K., 3, 8-12, 17, 105, 110
Sapp, M., 32
Savage, J., 34
Sawyer, J., 31
Schofield, J., 2, 19, 26, 36, 61, 62, 101, 106-107, 109
Schwartz, L., 2, 13, 17
Schwartzman, H., 75
Schweitzer, S., 62
Selman, R., 67, 75
Semaj, L., 1, 37, 44, 47, 51, 53
Shapiro, E., 26, 30, 107
Sherif, M., 63
Sherif, R., 63
Sigelman, L., 59-61, 77
Silberman, C., 32
Silk, A., 3, 13
Simon, B., 61
Singh, B., 26, 30
Singleton, L., 1, 2
Skerry, S., 59, 61, 100, 104, 108
Slaughter, D., 53
Slavin, R., 19, 26, 30, 107
Smith, D., 33
Smith, E., 40
Smith, R., 64
Smith, S., 25, 80
Snyder, H., 2, 107
Speier, M., 12
Spencer, M., 1, 37, 41, 44, 47-48, 51, 53, 59-60, 62-63, 85-86, 100-102, 104, 108-109
Spradley, J., 3, 12, 14, 105
Stephan, C., 85, 86, 101
Stephan, W., 26, 85, 86, 101, 106
St. John, N., 2, 25
Stroman, C., 65
Sutton-Smith, B., 92
Swap, W., 31

Tajfel, H., 40, 41
Taylor, A., 2, 106
Taylor, D., 19, 25, 26, 60
Taylor, R., 85
Teixeira, R., 26, 76, 78, 80, 106, 107, 109
Thomas, G., 3, 13
Thompson, R., 4
Turner, V., 12, 13, 92, 110
Tyler, S., 12

U.S. Government, Bureau of the Census, 20, 21

Van Evra, J., 63, 64, 110
Vega, W., 60

Waksler, F., 17
Warheit, G., 60
Weissbach, T., 101
Welch, S., 59-61, 77
Wellman, H., 48
Wiegel, J., 33
Wooley, J., 48
White, B., 63
White, M., 51, 62
Whitley, B., 2
Wieseman, R., 46, 108
Wilder, D., 40, 41, 54, 61, 62, 64, 65, 80
Williams, J., 1, 4, 38, 41, 63, 98, 108
Williams, R., 31
Wilson, A., 18
Wilson, M., 44, 54
Worchel, S., 25, 26, 61

Zajonc, R., 31, 104
Zigler, E., 31
Zimmerman, R., 60

Subject Index

Bryant School, 21-22

Categories:
  forming concepts of in and outgroup, 61-62, 109
  friend, 70-72
  gender, 34-37
  people, 40-46, 108-109
  prototypes for friend, 67-68
  prototypes for people, 42, 46
  prototypes for skin color, 98-99

Childbirth:
  children's knowledge of, 88-93
  mommy having a baby and, 90 (figure)
  mommy having a baby in the hospital and, 92 (figure)
  parental skin color and. *See Procreation*
Coles, Robert, 3
Conceptions of others:
  African American views and, 59-60
  distinguishing groups from individuals and, 61
  European American views and, 62
  factors that affect the children's, 60
Concord Elementary School, 22
Constructs:
  arbitrary ethnic and racial, 6n
  children's folk terms for people and, 41
  dualistic, 34-40
  social, 40-46
Corsaro, William, 75
Culture:
  definition of, 4
  school, 24-27

Data collection. *See* Methods

Elementary schools, 21-24
  culture of, 24-27
  household compositions and, 24
  locales, 20-21, 24
  racial variability in the, 25
  See also Field sites
Ethnic group, definition of, 4
Ethnic identity, definition of, 4-5

Field sites, 20-24
  gaining access to, 9-10
  selection of, 7-8
Friends:
  boy/girlfriends, 81-83
  categories of, 70-72
  definitions of, 66-68
  interracial "best friends," 77 (figure)
  investigator's "special," 15-17
  making, 75-76
  race as a factor in selecting, 68-69, 79
  ranking, 72-73
  seating arrangements and the influence on making, 27-30
  selection process for, 68, 78-81
  See also "Romantic" relationships

Friendship:
forming, 76-78
organizing principles, 67-69
rules of, 74-75

Gesell, Arnold, 66
Goodenough, Ward, 4, 12

Identity:
gender, 34-36, 47
racial, 37, 44, 47, 51, 53, 109

Joseph School, 23-24

Kindergarten, 31-33
classrooms, 27, 28 (figure), 29 (figure), 30-31
curriculum, 32

Lawrence School, 22-23

Methods, 3, 4, 7-19, 105
informants. *See also* Investigator's "special" friends
investigator's relationship with the children as, 10-12
participant observation and, 12-13
problems and solutions, 17-19
shallow cover and, 10

Piaget, Jean, 2, 5, 40, 47, 109
Prejudice:
desegregation and reducing. *See* Racial harmony at school
European American children and, 63-64
factors affecting, 54
interracial couples and, 83-86
Procreation, parent-child resemblance, skin color and, 93-101

Race, definition of, 4
Racial attitudes, 106-107
adult involvement and, 46, 65, 86, 104, 108-109
and the effects of the media on, 64-65, 85, 110
parents' role in shaping, 53-54, 85-86, 110

Racial harmony:
at school, 24-27, 31, 80, 106-107
children's solutions for maintaining, 54, 105-106
teacher intervention and effects of seating patterns on, 31
Racial integration. *See* Racial harmony
Racial relationships, 75-76
effects of assimilation and accommodation on, 109-110
effects of classroom seating patterns on, 30-31, 80
effects of curriculum on, 24-27
See also Friends
"Romantic" relationships:
boy/girl friends, 81-83
children's subjective feelings about interracial, 101-104
race and its effects on the selection process of, 83-86
Rosch, Eleanor, 67

Schofield, Janet, 61
Self-conceptions, 44, 47-58, 93
colors black and white and, 37
friendship and, 68
social comparisons and, 40-41
Self-portraits:
by Dicky, 56 (figure)
by Doug, 52 (figure)
by Greg, 57 (figure)
by Julie, 51 (figure)
by Maria, 50 (figure)
by Michele, 49 (figure)
descriptions of, 48-55
differences between European American and African American children's, 48-55
Settings. *See* Elementary schools
Social cognition:
categories of people and, 40-46, 108-109
See also Categories of friends
Spencer, Margaret, 60

Theoretical stance, 12
Thoreau School, 23

About the Author

Robyn M. Holmes is Assistant Professor of Psychology at Monmouth College, New Jersey. Her general interest is in child development and behavior, with a specialization in children's racial beliefs and play. In addition to *How Young Children Perceive Race,* she has written articles in such interdisciplinary journals as *Play & Culture* and *Child Study Journal.* She is a Fellow of the American Anthropological Association and a member of the American Psychological Society and the Association for the Study of Play. She received her Ph.D. in anthropology from Rutgers University.